31.00

GRAPHIC PREHISTORIC ANIMALS

GIANT SLOTH
MEGATHERIUM

ILLUSTRATED BY ALESSANDRO POLUZZI

Smart Apple Media

Published by Smart Apple Media, an imprint of Black Rabbit Books
P.O. Box 3263, Mankato, Minnesota 56002
www.blackrabbitbooks.com

U.S. publication copyright © 2017 Smart Apple Media. International copyright reserved in all countries. No part of this book may be reproduced in any form without written permission from the publisher.

Produced by David West Children's Books
6 Princeton Court, 55 Felsham Road, London SW15 1AZ

Designed and written by Gary Jeffrey

Copyright © 2017 David West Children's Books

Cataloging-in-Publication data is on file with the Library of Congress.
ISBN 978-1-62588-409-1
eBook ISBN 978-1-62588-425-1

Printed in China
CPSIA compliance information: DWCB16CP
010116

9 8 7 6 5 4 3 2 1

CONTENTS

WHAT IS A GIANT SLOTH?
Learn the facts about this amazing animal.
page 4

THE STORY...
GIANT SLOTH IN THE ICE AGE WOODS OF SOUTH AMERICA
page 6

FOSSIL FINDS
Find out about amazing giant sloth remains.
page 22

ANIMAL GALLERY
Look up the animals that appear in the story.
page 23

GLOSSARY AND INDEX
page 24

WHAT IS A GIANT SLOTH?

MEGATHERIUM MEANS "GREAT BEAST"

Megatherium was the biggest of the giant sloths and lived 2 million to 10,000 years ago, during the **Pleistocene period**. **Fossils** of its skeletons have been found in South America and North America (see page 22).

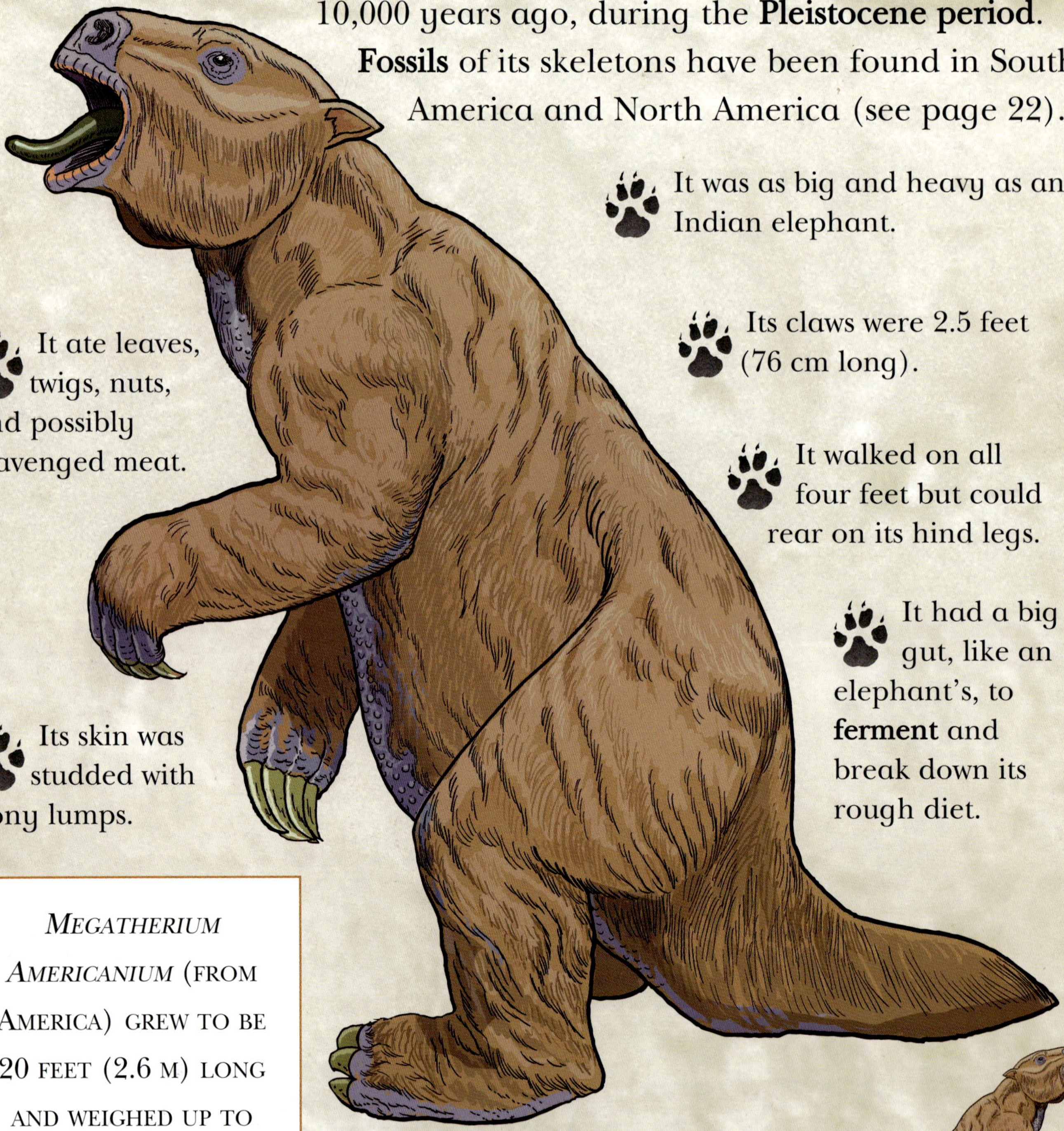

- It was as big and heavy as an Indian elephant.
- Its claws were 2.5 feet (76 cm long).
- It walked on all four feet but could rear on its hind legs.
- It had a big gut, like an elephant's, to **ferment** and break down its rough diet.
- It ate leaves, twigs, nuts, and possibly scavenged meat.
- Its skin was studded with bony lumps.
- It walked on the sides of its feet.

Megatherium americanium (from America) grew to be 20 feet (2.6 m) long and weighed up to 3 tons (2,722 kg).

This would be *Megatherium* and you.

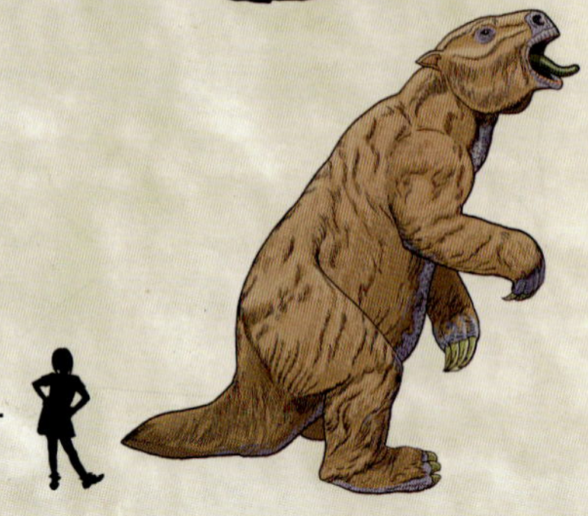

ANIMAL FACTS

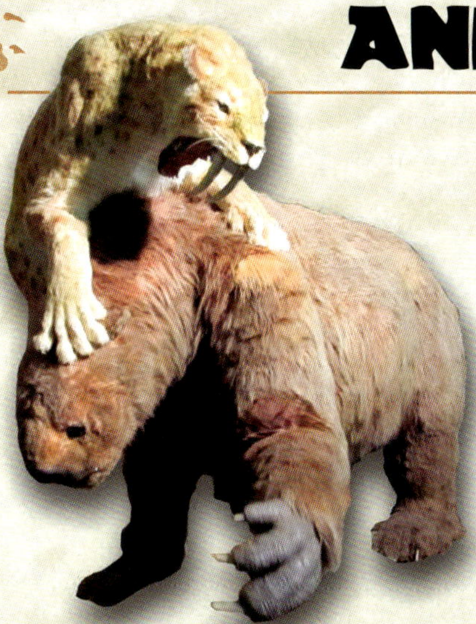

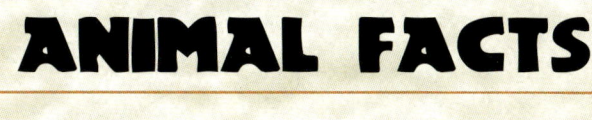

The smaller giant ground sloth species were at the mercy of ice age ***predators****, such as the sabertooth cat.*

Giant sloths first appeared 23 million years ago in South America when it was a separate continent. They had huge bones and joints and evolved to be massively strong. The biggest were **browsers** and stood upright. They used their fat tails to steady themselves so they could reach up high to the biggest branches.

Because of their size, strength, and fearsome claws, the biggest giant sloths had no natural predators. If they were attacked, the **osteoderms** in their skin acted like **chainmail** armor.

Some scientists think giant sloths might have chased meat eaters away from their kills during times of famine. Although they moved slowly, few animals would want to risk getting in the way of a wandering *Megatherium*.

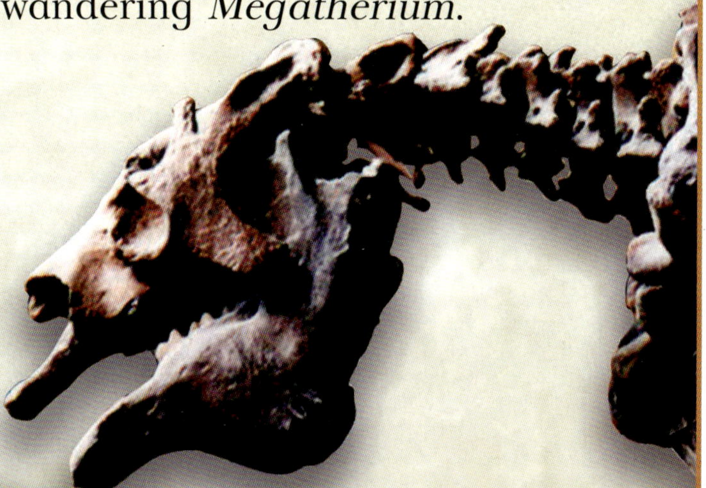

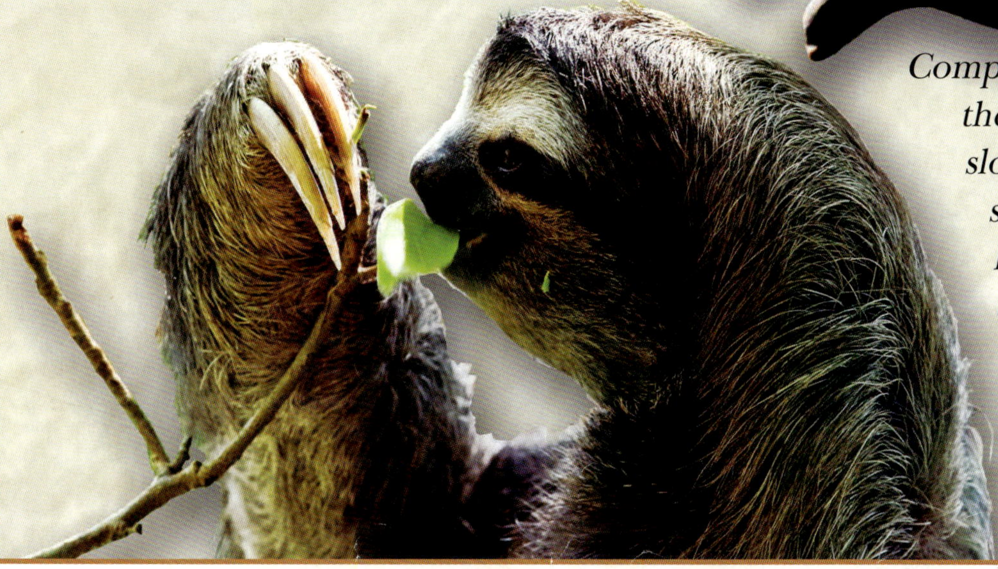

Compared with Megatherium, *the modern-day three-toed sloth (left) is tiny. Today's sloth avoids predators by living in trees and rarely touches the ground. The skeletons of giant sloths (above) show that they looked very different from today's sloths.*

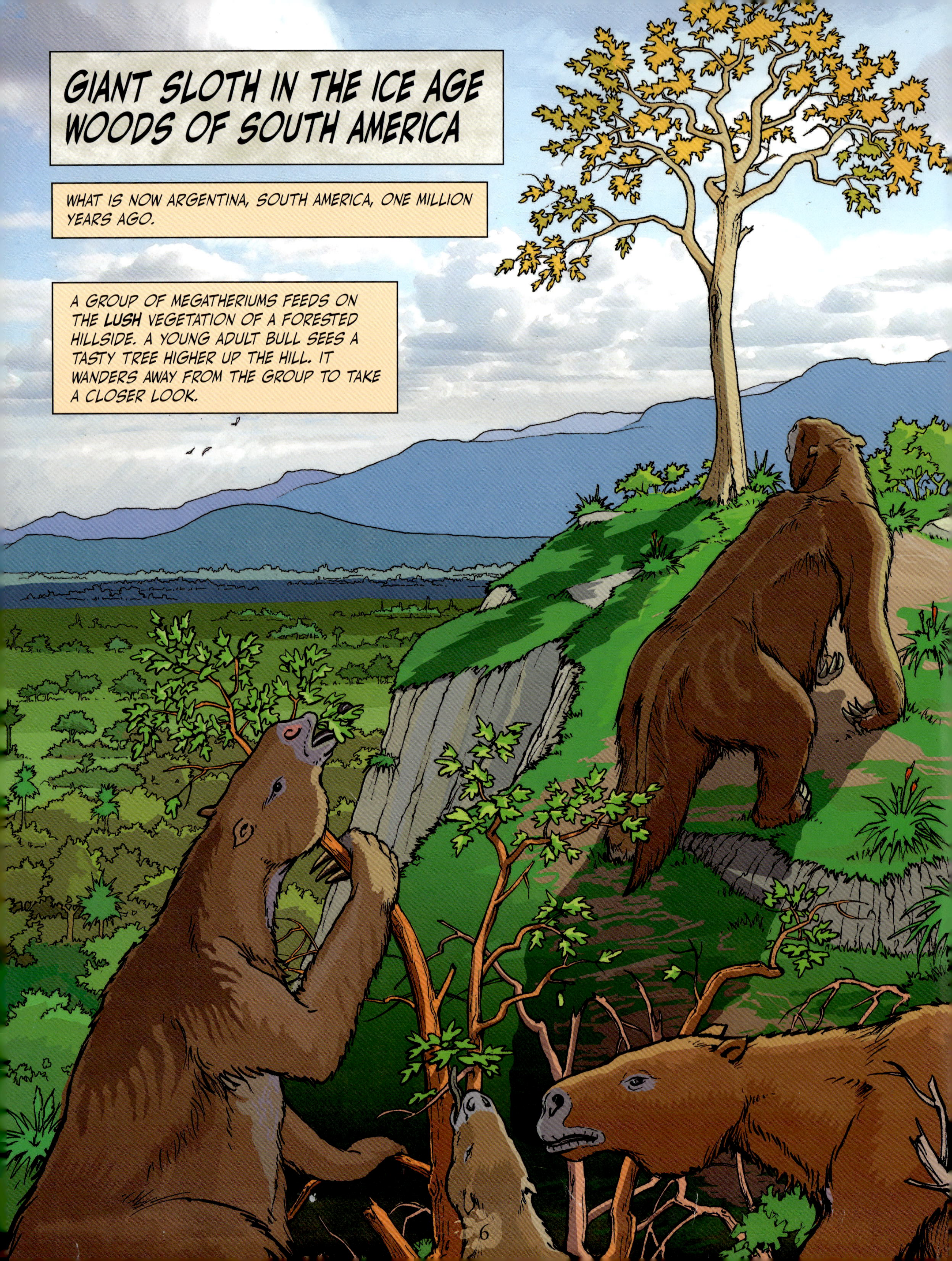
GIANT SLOTH IN THE ICE AGE WOODS OF SOUTH AMERICA
WHAT IS NOW ARGENTINA, SOUTH AMERICA, ONE MILLION YEARS AGO.
A GROUP OF MEGATHERIUMS FEEDS ON THE LUSH VEGETATION OF A FORESTED HILLSIDE. A YOUNG ADULT BULL SEES A TASTY TREE HIGHER UP THE HILL. IT WANDERS AWAY FROM THE GROUP TO TAKE A CLOSER LOOK.

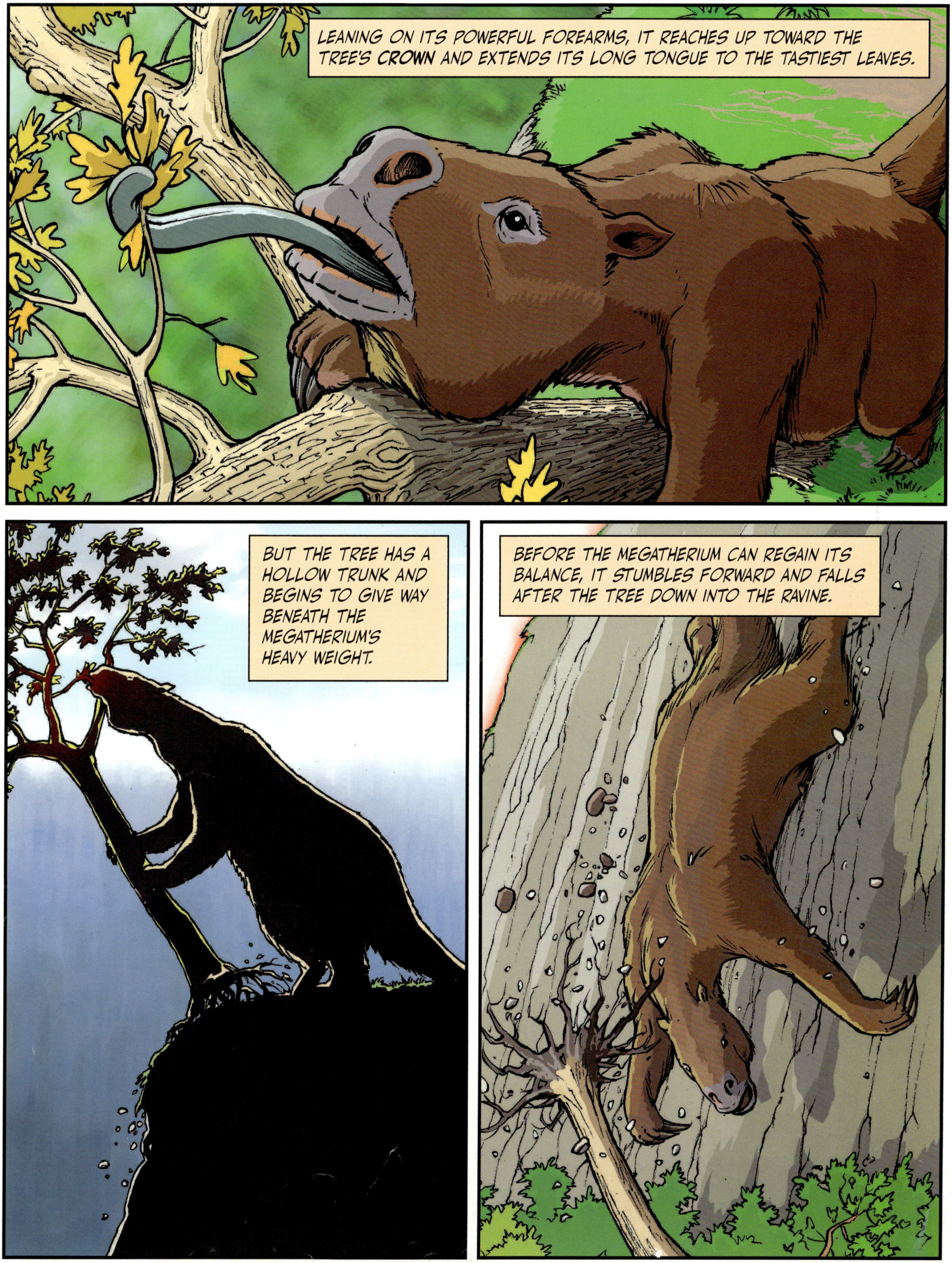
LEANING ON ITS POWERFUL FOREARMS, IT REACHES UP TOWARD THE TREE'S **CROWN** AND EXTENDS ITS LONG TONGUE TO THE TASTIEST LEAVES.
BUT THE TREE HAS A HOLLOW TRUNK AND BEGINS TO GIVE WAY BENEATH THE MEGATHERIUM'S HEAVY WEIGHT.
BEFORE THE MEGATHERIUM CAN REGAIN ITS BALANCE, IT STUMBLES FORWARD AND FALLS AFTER THE TREE DOWN INTO THE RAVINE.

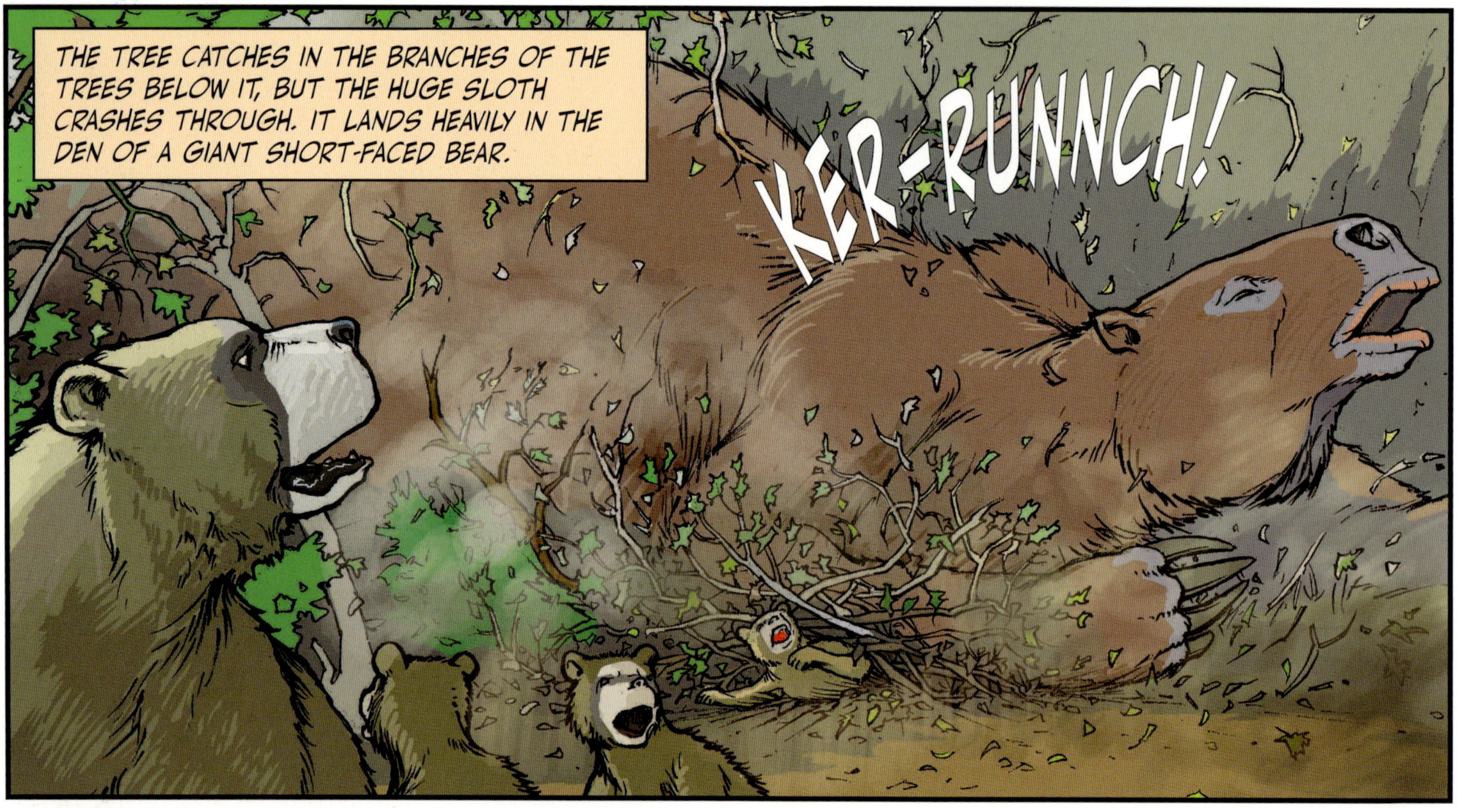
THE TREE CATCHES IN THE BRANCHES OF THE TREES BELOW IT, BUT THE HUGE SLOTH CRASHES THROUGH. IT LANDS HEAVILY IN THE DEN OF A GIANT SHORT-FACED BEAR.
KER-RUNNCH!

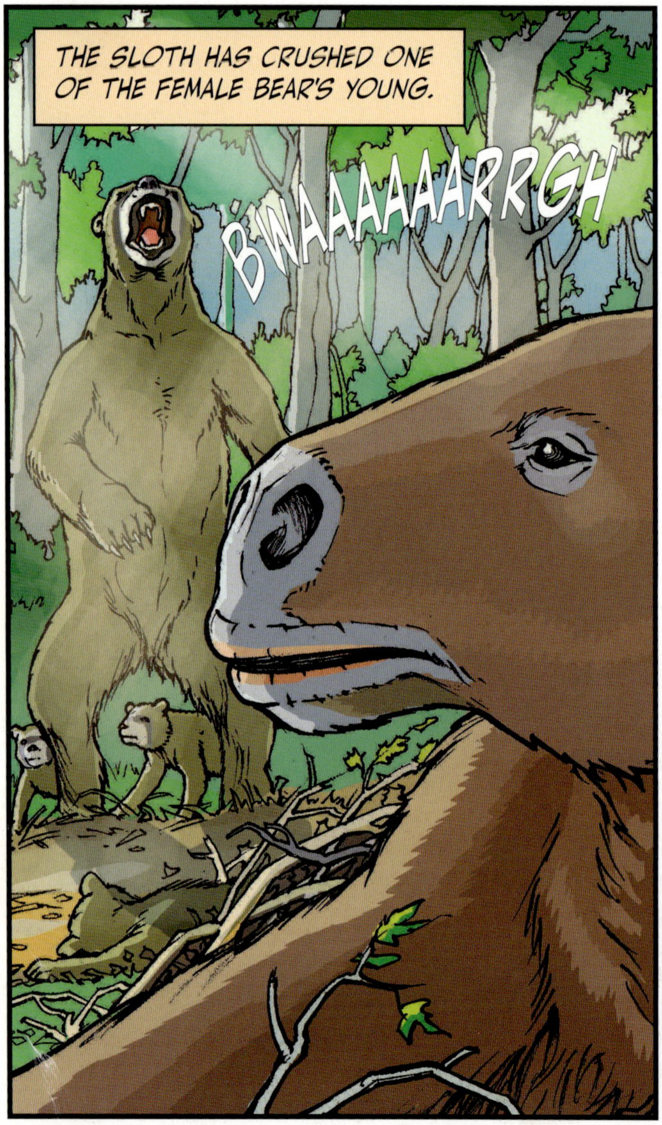
THE SLOTH HAS CRUSHED ONE OF THE FEMALE BEAR'S YOUNG.
BWAAAAAARRGH

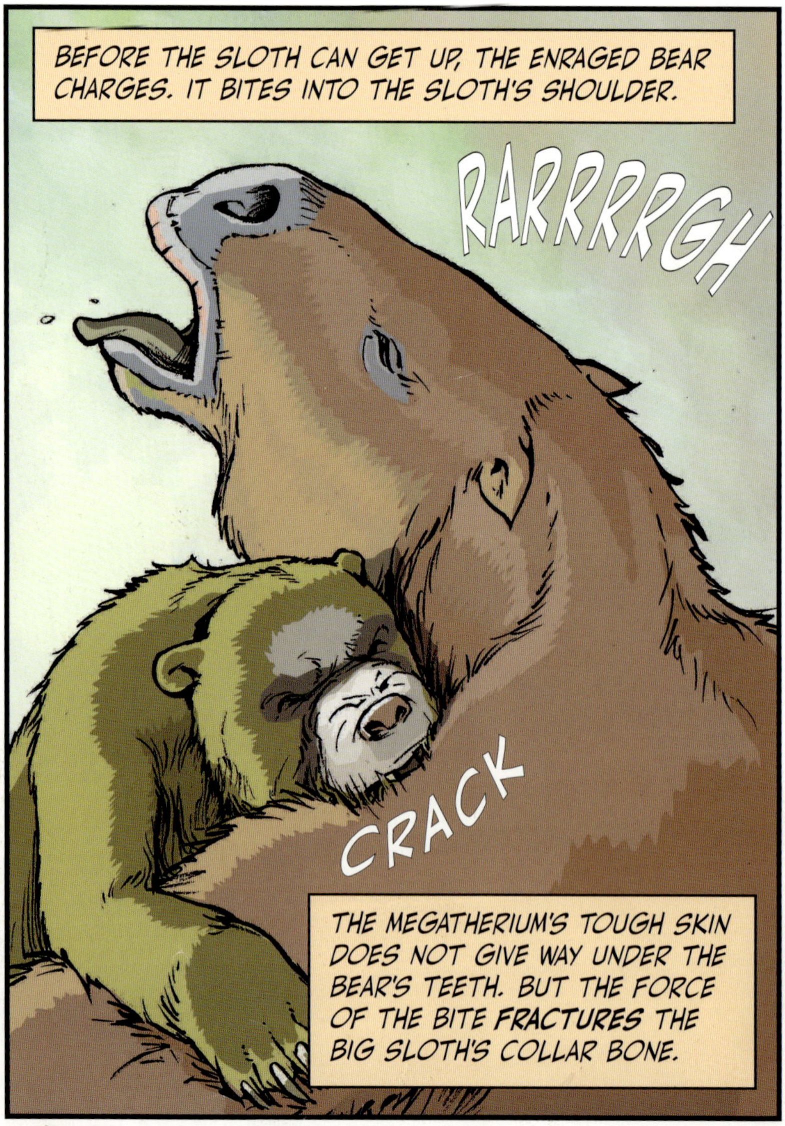
BEFORE THE SLOTH CAN GET UP, THE ENRAGED BEAR CHARGES. IT BITES INTO THE SLOTH'S SHOULDER.
RARRRRGH
CRACK
THE MEGATHERIUM'S TOUGH SKIN DOES NOT GIVE WAY UNDER THE BEAR'S TEETH. BUT THE FORCE OF THE BITE **FRACTURES** THE BIG SLOTH'S COLLAR BONE.

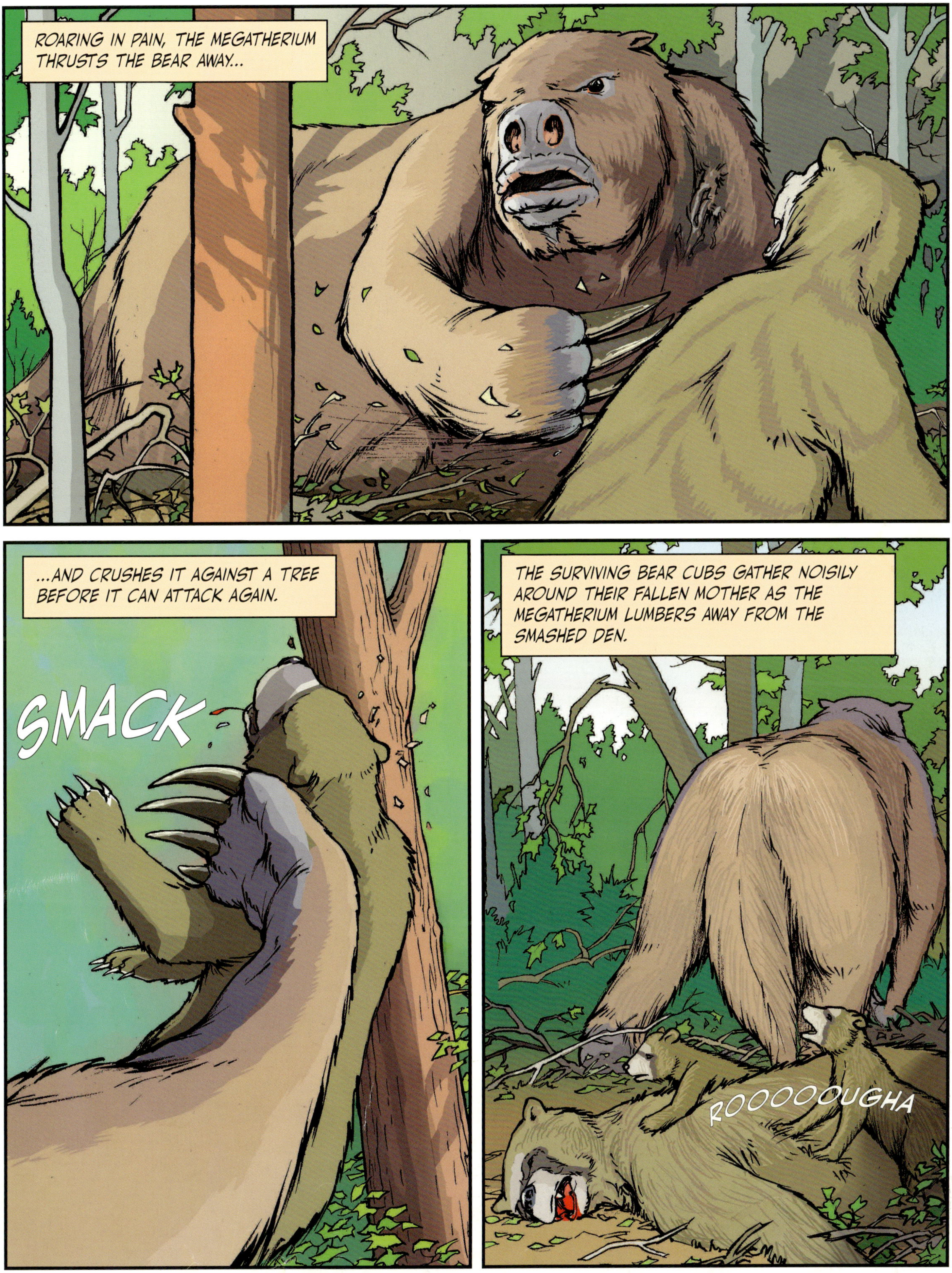
ROARING IN PAIN, THE MEGATHERIUM THRUSTS THE BEAR AWAY...
...AND CRUSHES IT AGAINST A TREE BEFORE IT CAN ATTACK AGAIN.
SMACK
THE SURVIVING BEAR CUBS GATHER NOISILY AROUND THEIR FALLEN MOTHER AS THE MEGATHERIUM LUMBERS AWAY FROM THE SMASHED DEN.
ROOOOOUGHA

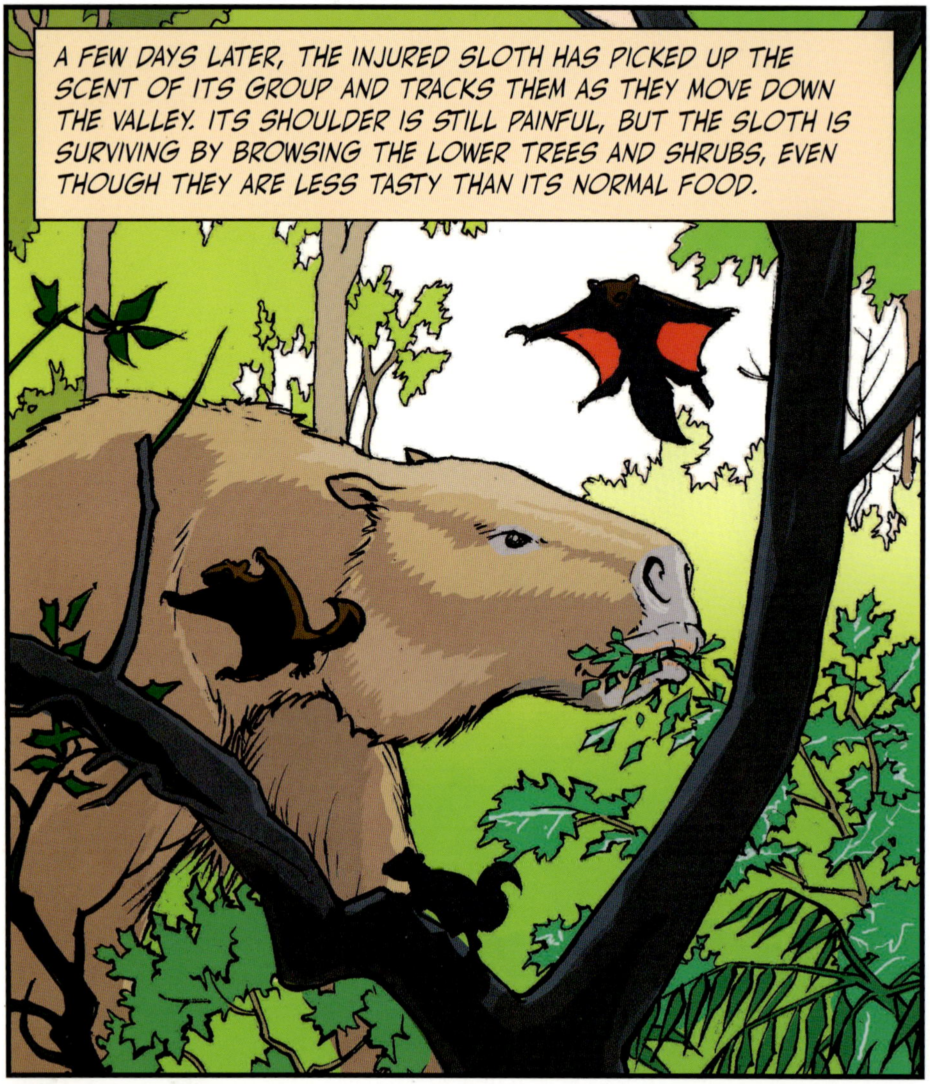
A FEW DAYS LATER, THE INJURED SLOTH HAS PICKED UP THE SCENT OF ITS GROUP AND TRACKS THEM AS THEY MOVE DOWN THE VALLEY. ITS SHOULDER IS STILL PAINFUL, BUT THE SLOTH IS SURVIVING BY BROWSING THE LOWER TREES AND SHRUBS, EVEN THOUGH THEY ARE LESS TASTY THAN ITS NORMAL FOOD.

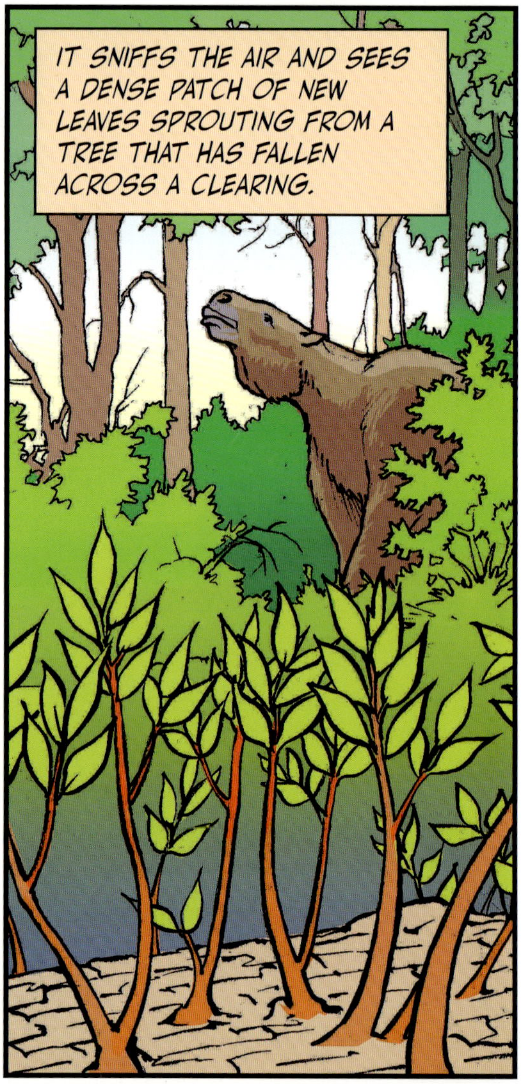
IT SNIFFS THE AIR AND SEES A DENSE PATCH OF NEW LEAVES SPROUTING FROM A TREE THAT HAS FALLEN ACROSS A CLEARING.

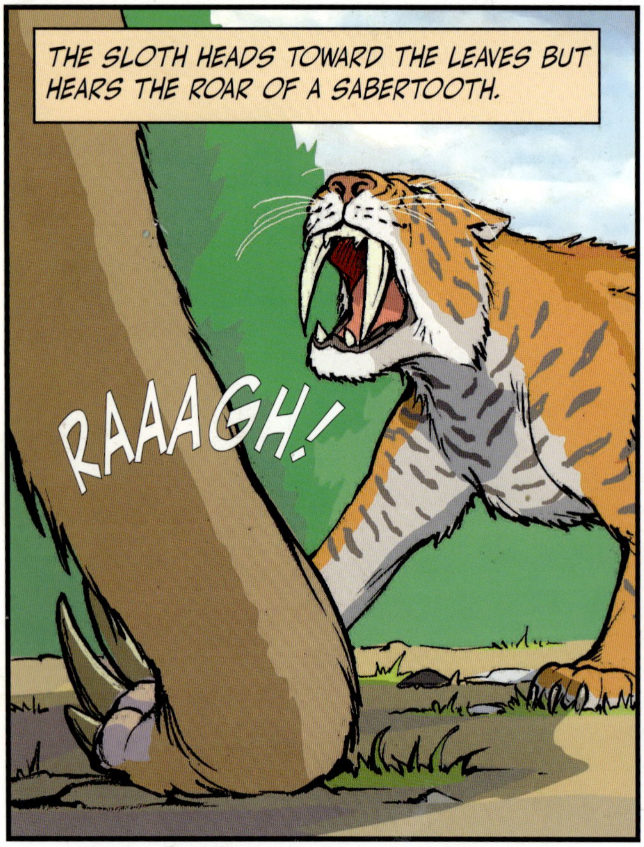
THE SLOTH HEADS TOWARD THE LEAVES BUT HEARS THE ROAR OF A SABERTOOTH.
RAAAGH!

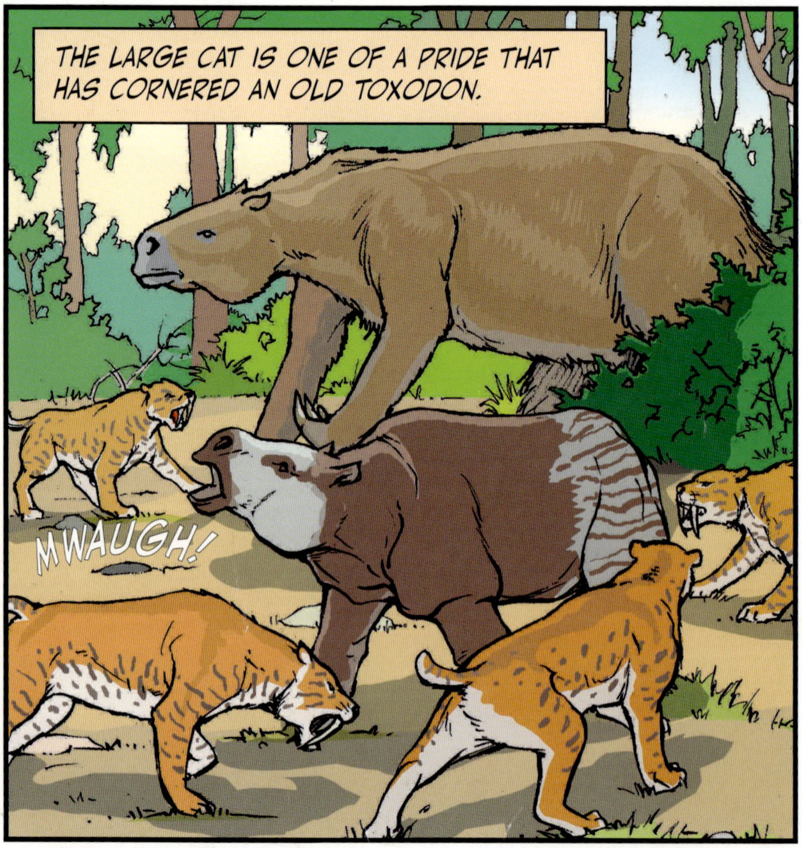
THE LARGE CAT IS ONE OF A PRIDE THAT HAS CORNERED AN OLD TOXODON.
MWAUGH!

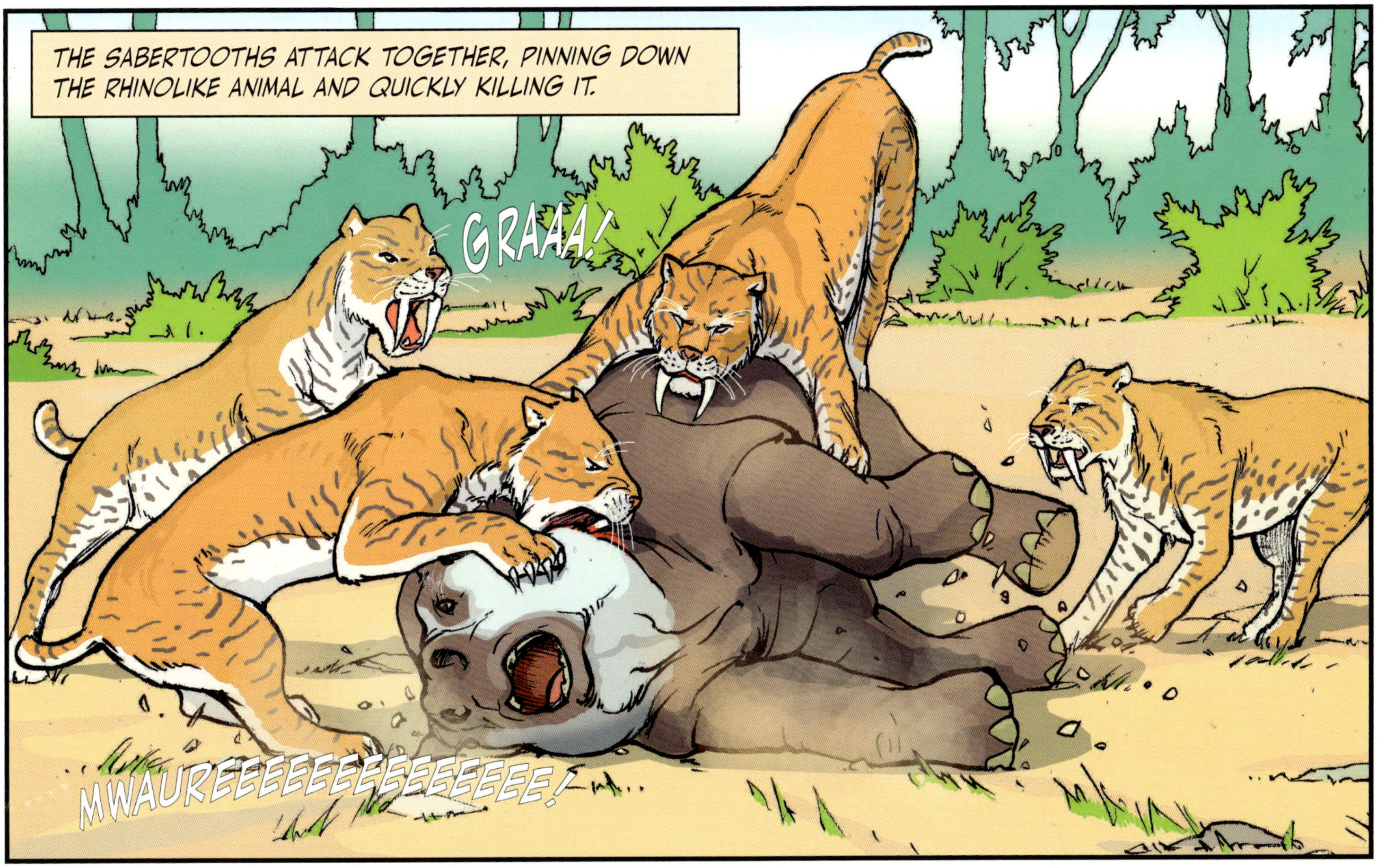
THE SABERTOOTHS ATTACK TOGETHER, PINNING DOWN THE RHINOLIKE ANIMAL AND QUICKLY KILLING IT.
GRAAA!
MWAUREEEEEEEEEEEEEEE!

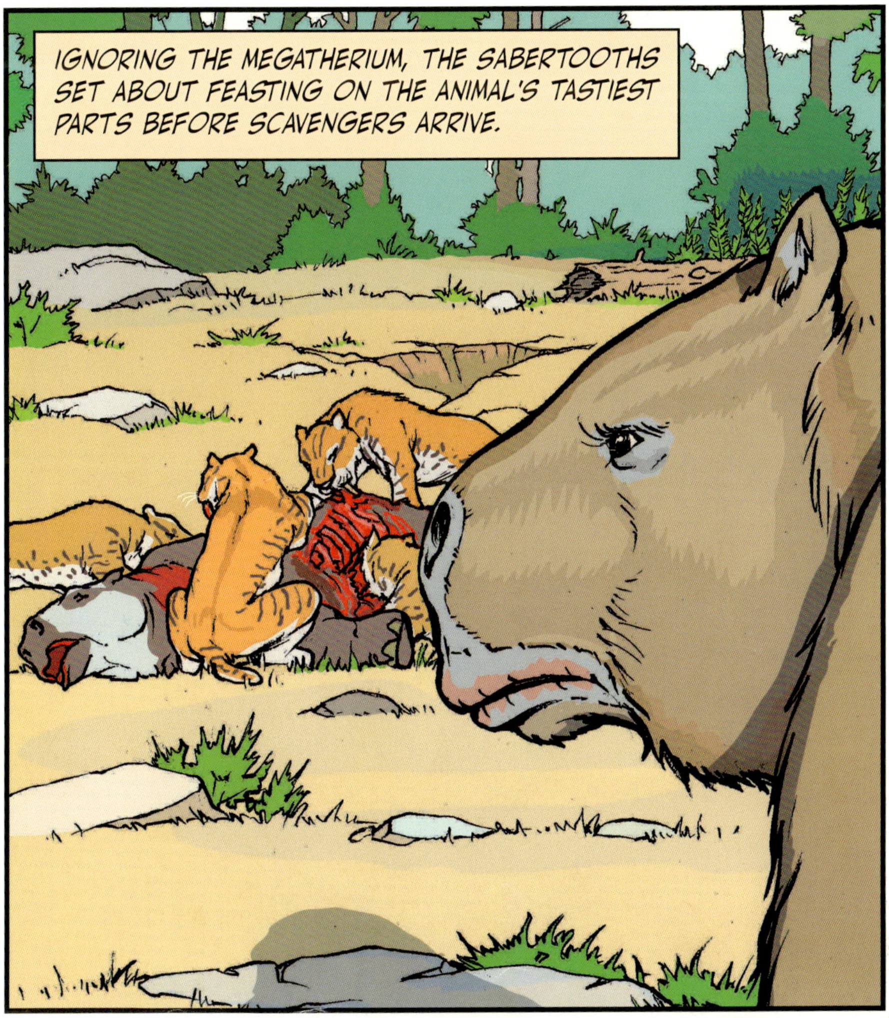
IGNORING THE MEGATHERIUM, THE SABERTOOTHS SET ABOUT FEASTING ON THE ANIMAL'S TASTIEST PARTS BEFORE SCAVENGERS ARRIVE.

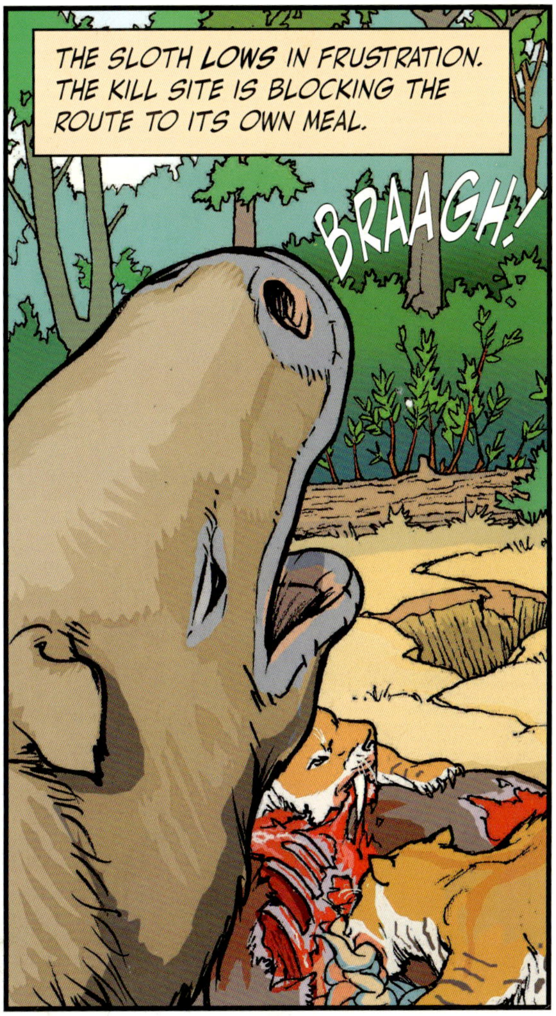
THE SLOTH **LOWS** IN FRUSTRATION. THE KILL SITE IS BLOCKING THE ROUTE TO ITS OWN MEAL.
BRAAGH!

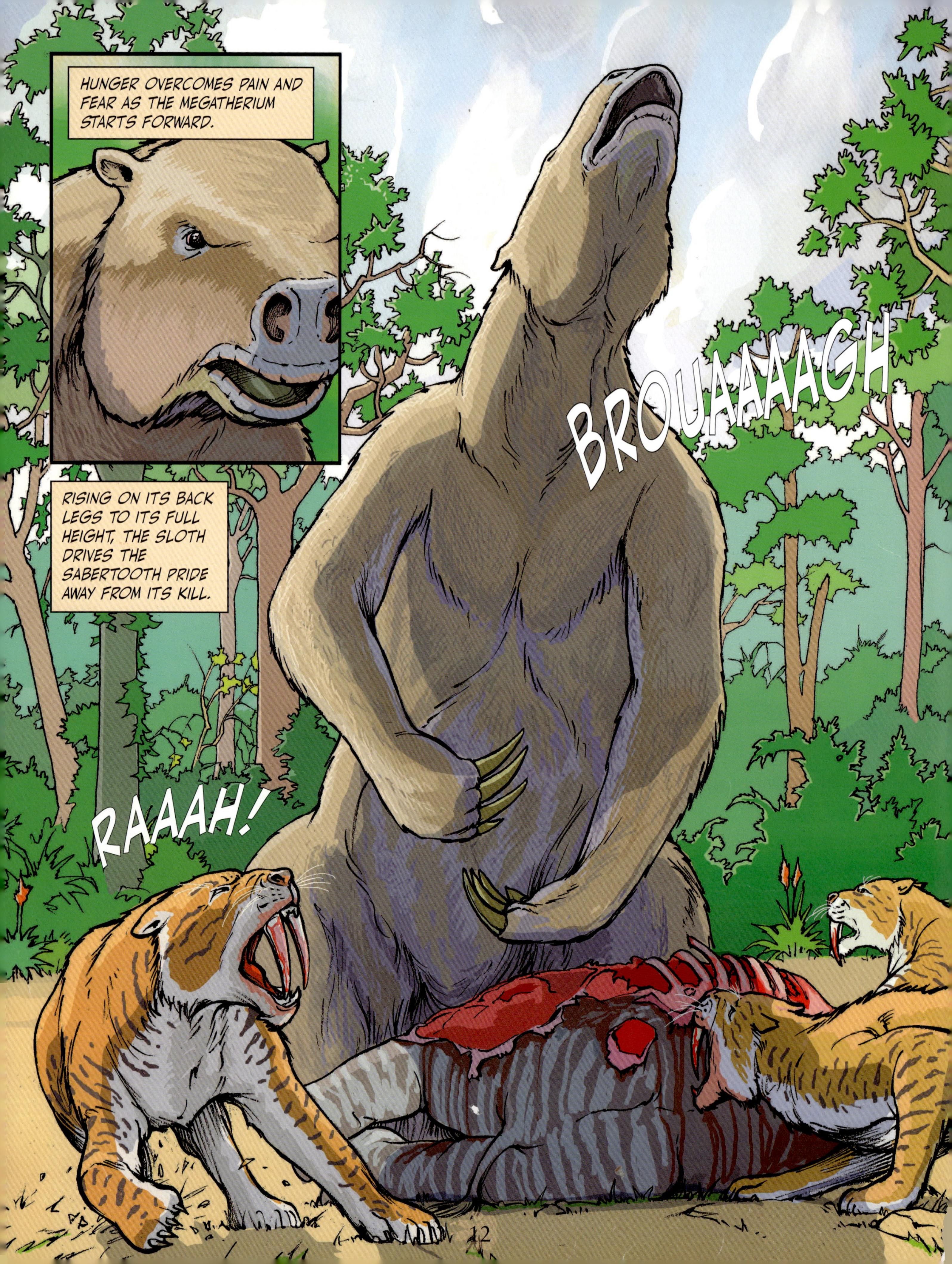
HUNGER OVERCOMES PAIN AND FEAR AS THE MEGATHERIUM STARTS FORWARD.
RISING ON ITS BACK LEGS TO ITS FULL HEIGHT, THE SLOTH DRIVES THE SABERTOOTH PRIDE AWAY FROM ITS KILL.
BROUAAAAGH
RAAAH!

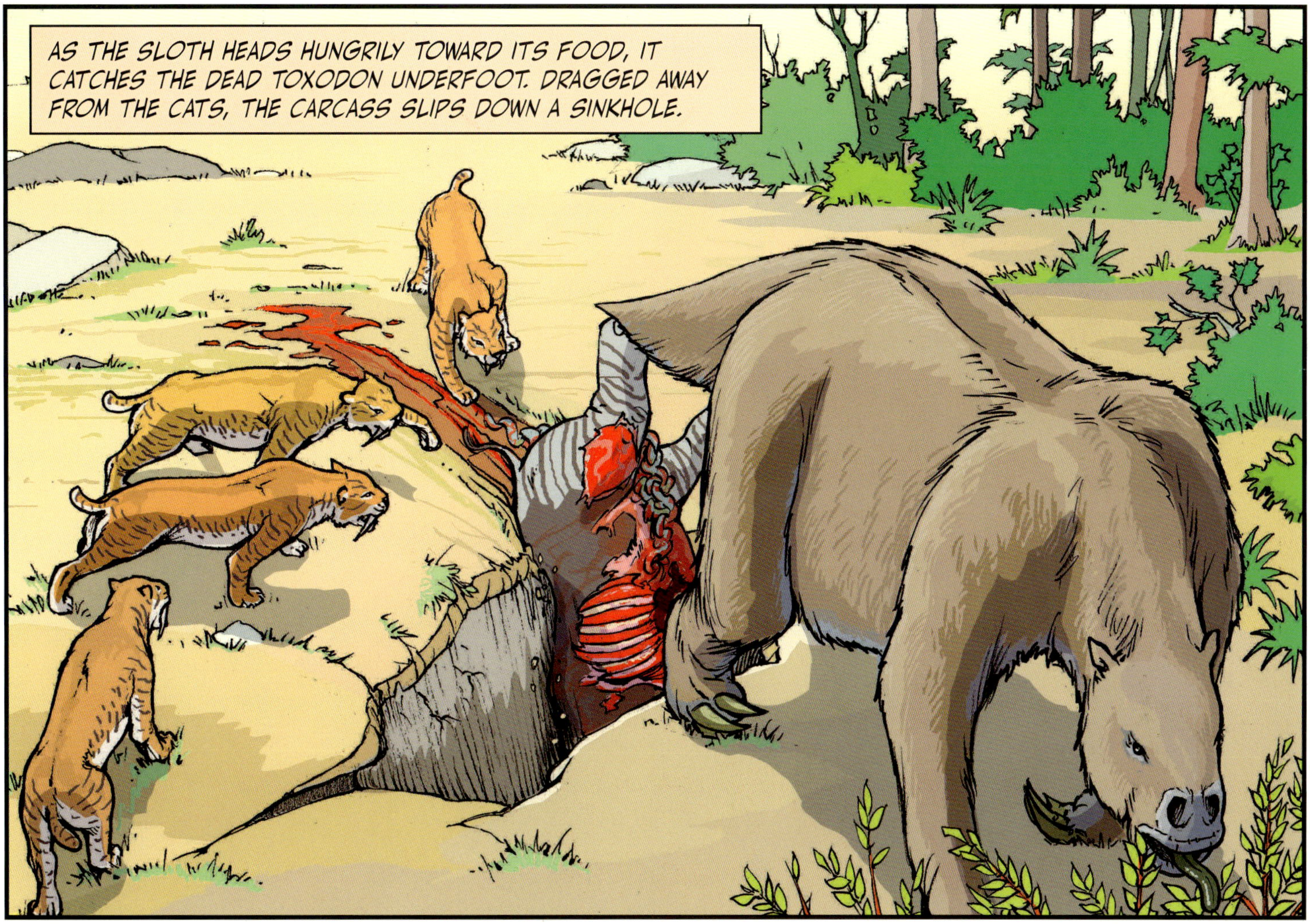
AS THE SLOTH HEADS HUNGRILY TOWARD ITS FOOD, IT CATCHES THE DEAD TOXODON UNDERFOOT. DRAGGED AWAY FROM THE CATS, THE CARCASS SLIPS DOWN A SINKHOLE.

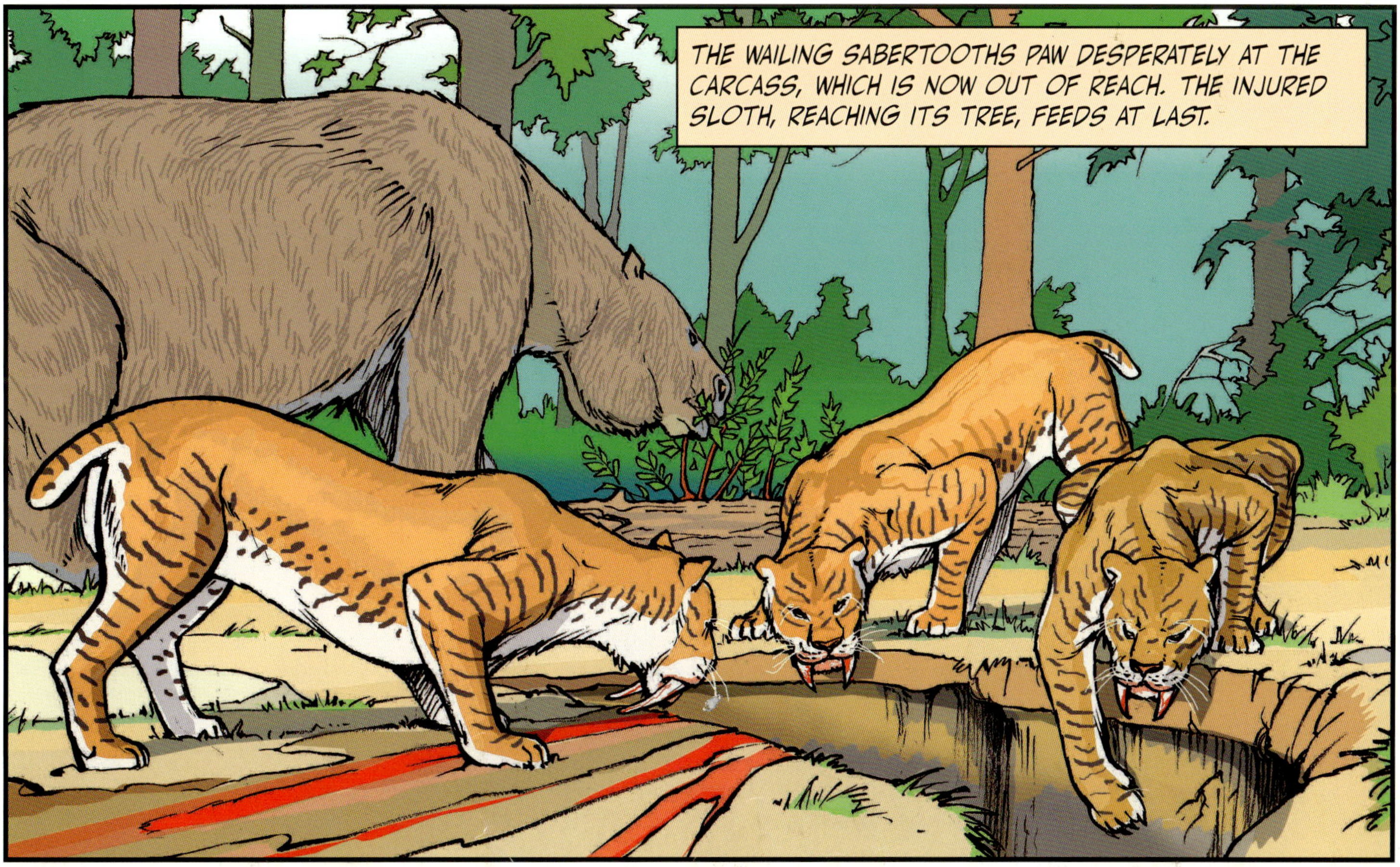
THE WAILING SABERTOOTHS PAW DESPERATELY AT THE CARCASS, WHICH IS NOW OUT OF REACH. THE INJURED SLOTH, REACHING ITS TREE, FEEDS AT LAST.

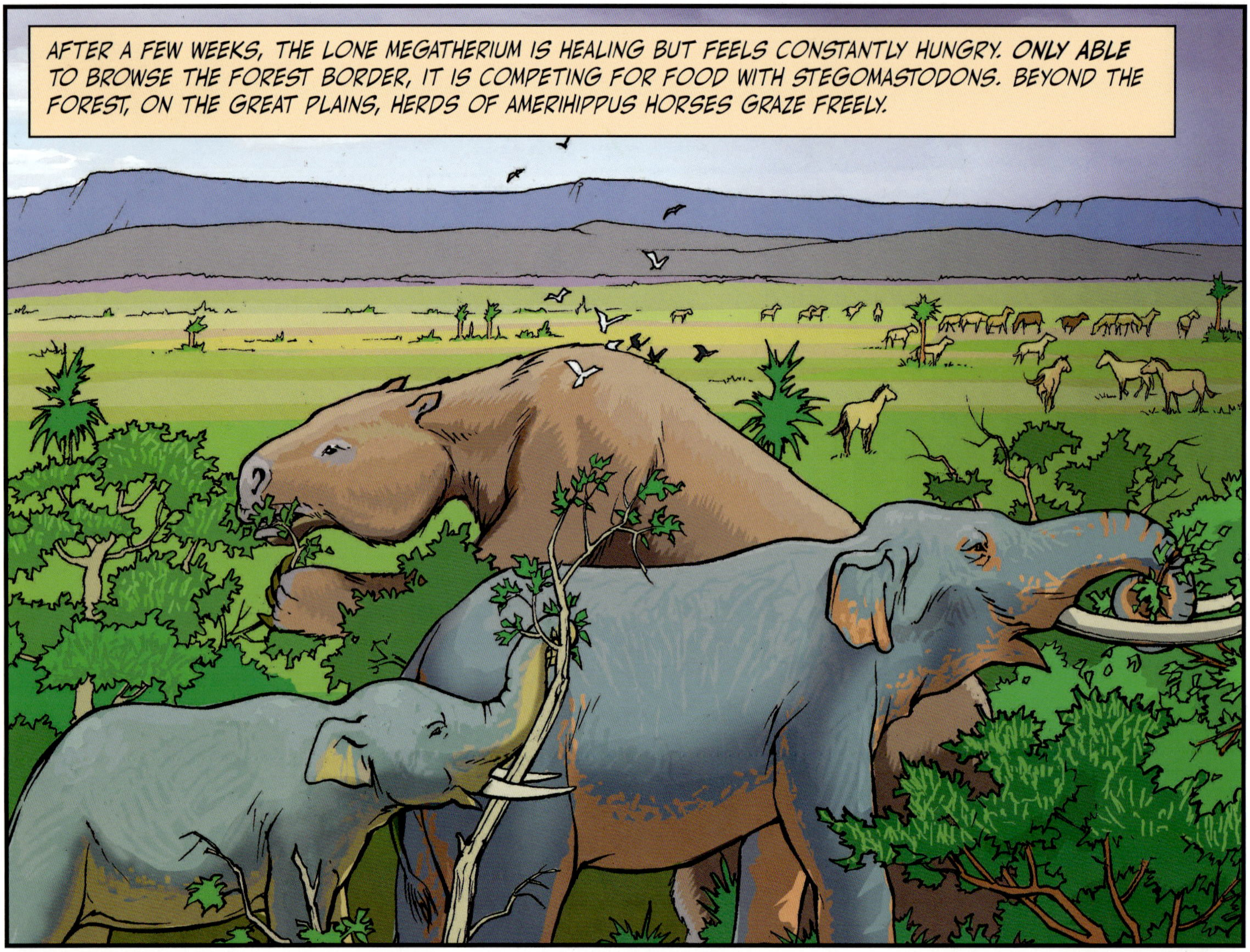
AFTER A FEW WEEKS, THE LONE MEGATHERIUM IS HEALING BUT FEELS CONSTANTLY HUNGRY. ONLY ABLE TO BROWSE THE FOREST BORDER, IT IS COMPETING FOR FOOD WITH STEGOMASTODONS. BEYOND THE FOREST, ON THE GREAT PLAINS, HERDS OF AMERIHIPPUS HORSES GRAZE FREELY.

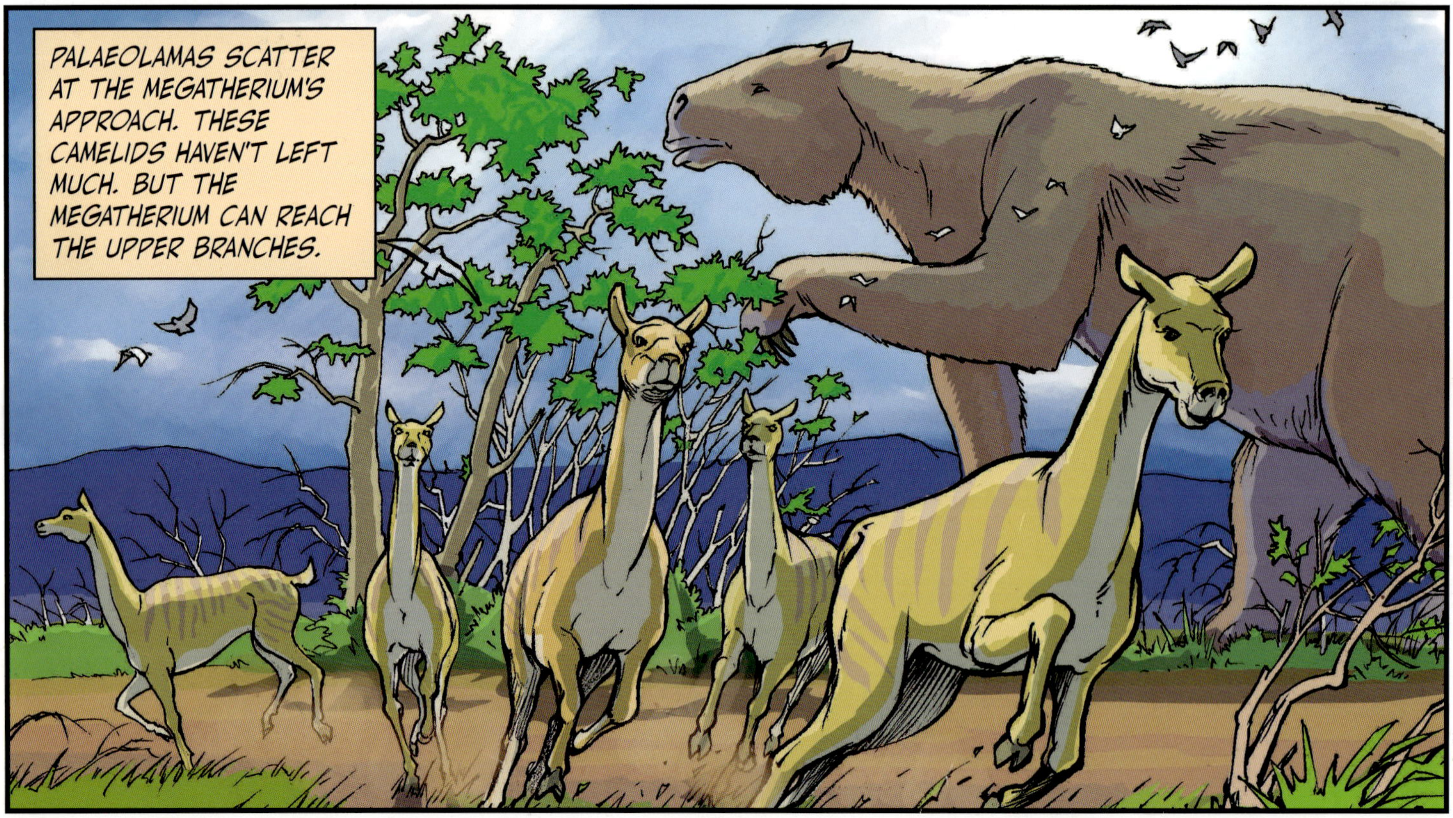
PALAEOLAMAS SCATTER AT THE MEGATHERIUM'S APPROACH. THESE CAMELIDS HAVEN'T LEFT MUCH. BUT THE MEGATHERIUM CAN REACH THE UPPER BRANCHES.

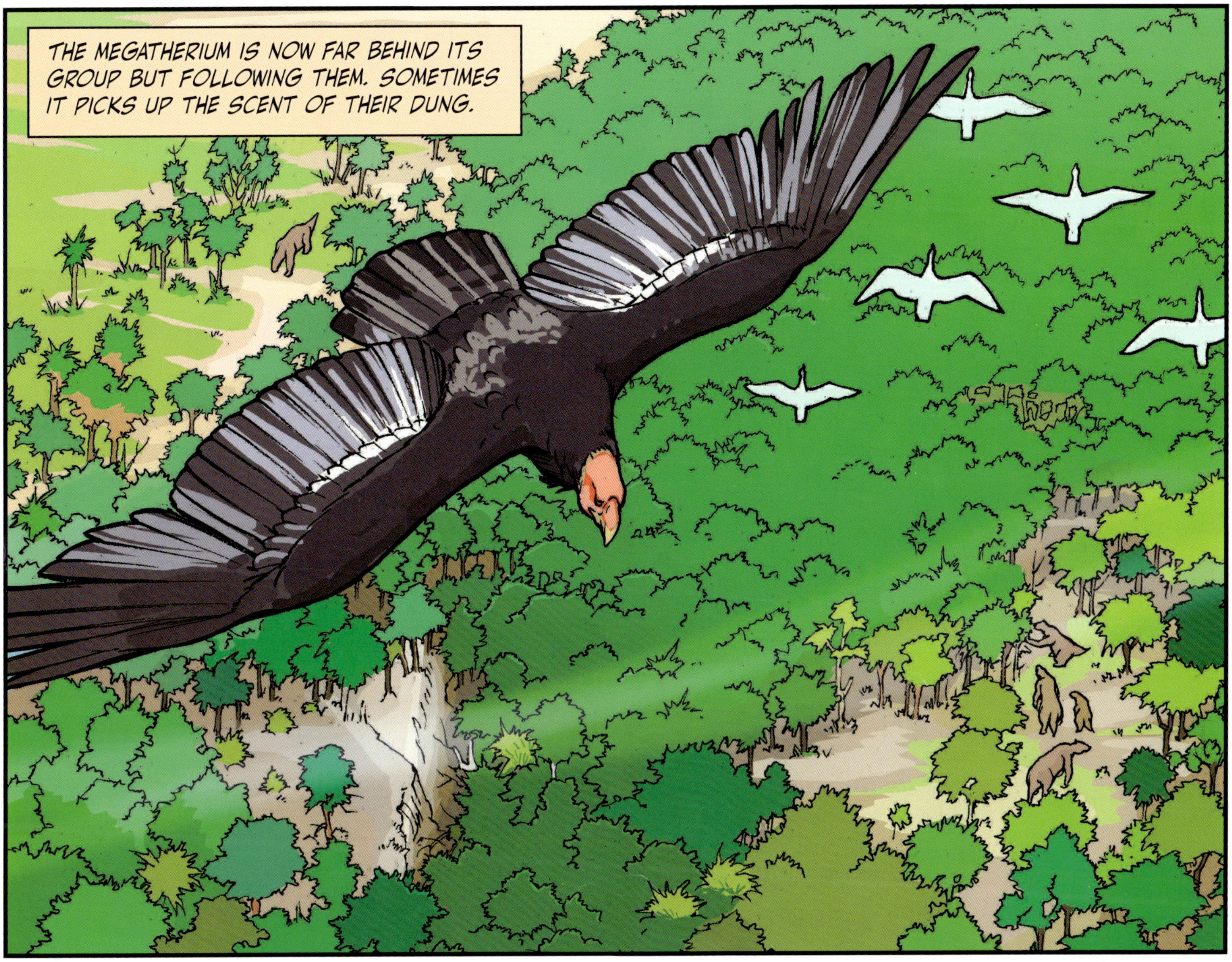
THE MEGATHERIUM IS NOW FAR BEHIND ITS GROUP BUT FOLLOWING THEM. SOMETIMES IT PICKS UP THE SCENT OF THEIR DUNG.

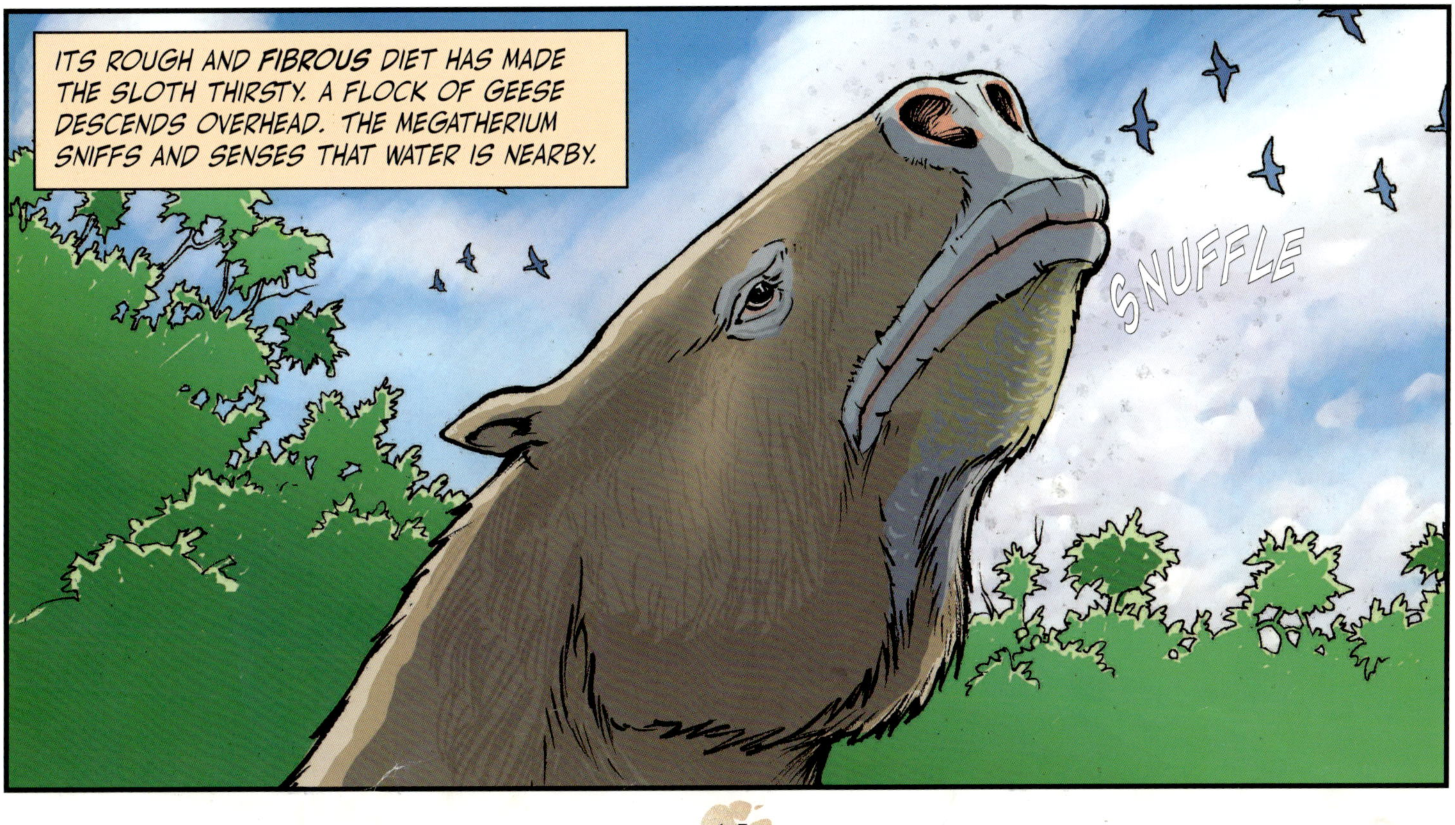
ITS ROUGH AND FIBROUS DIET HAS MADE THE SLOTH THIRSTY. A FLOCK OF GEESE DESCENDS OVERHEAD. THE MEGATHERIUM SNIFFS AND SENSES THAT WATER IS NEARBY.
SNUFFLE

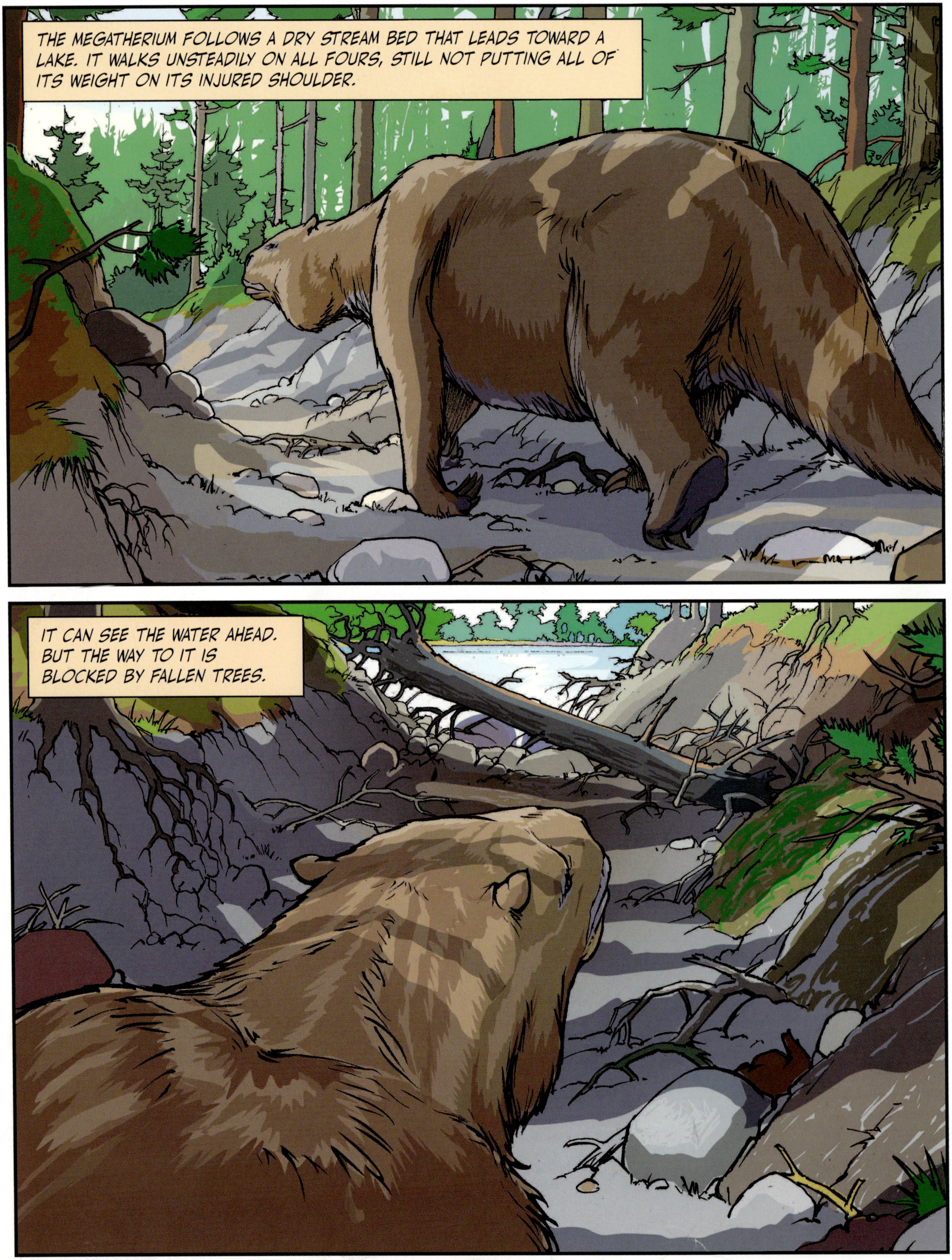
THE MEGATHERIUM FOLLOWS A DRY STREAM BED THAT LEADS TOWARD A LAKE. IT WALKS UNSTEADILY ON ALL FOURS, STILL NOT PUTTING ALL OF ITS WEIGHT ON ITS INJURED SHOULDER.
IT CAN SEE THE WATER AHEAD. BUT THE WAY TO IT IS BLOCKED BY FALLEN TREES.

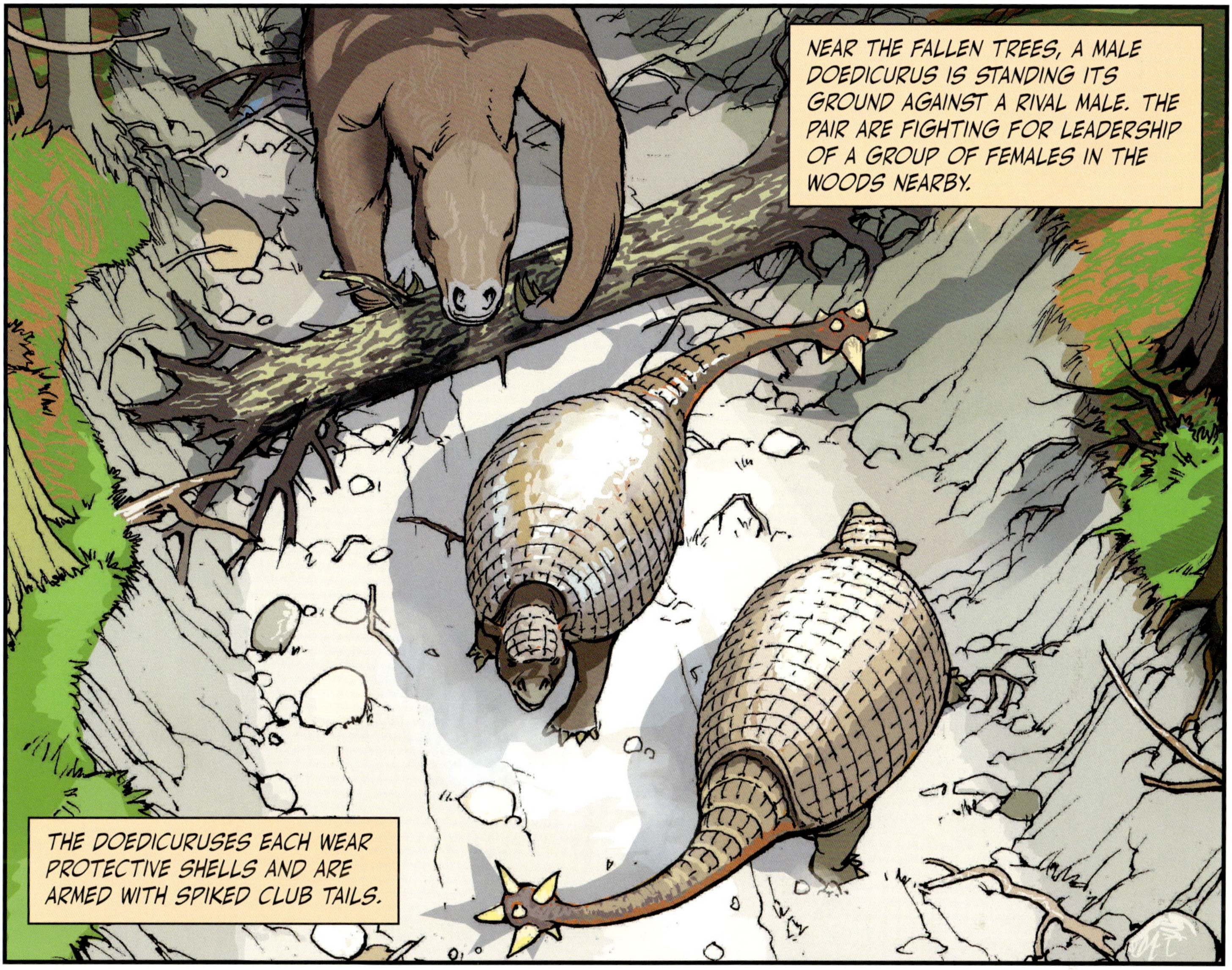
NEAR THE FALLEN TREES, A MALE DOEDICURUS IS STANDING ITS GROUND AGAINST A RIVAL MALE. THE PAIR ARE FIGHTING FOR LEADERSHIP OF A GROUP OF FEMALES IN THE WOODS NEARBY.
THE DOEDICURUSES EACH WEAR PROTECTIVE SHELLS AND ARE ARMED WITH SPIKED CLUB TAILS.

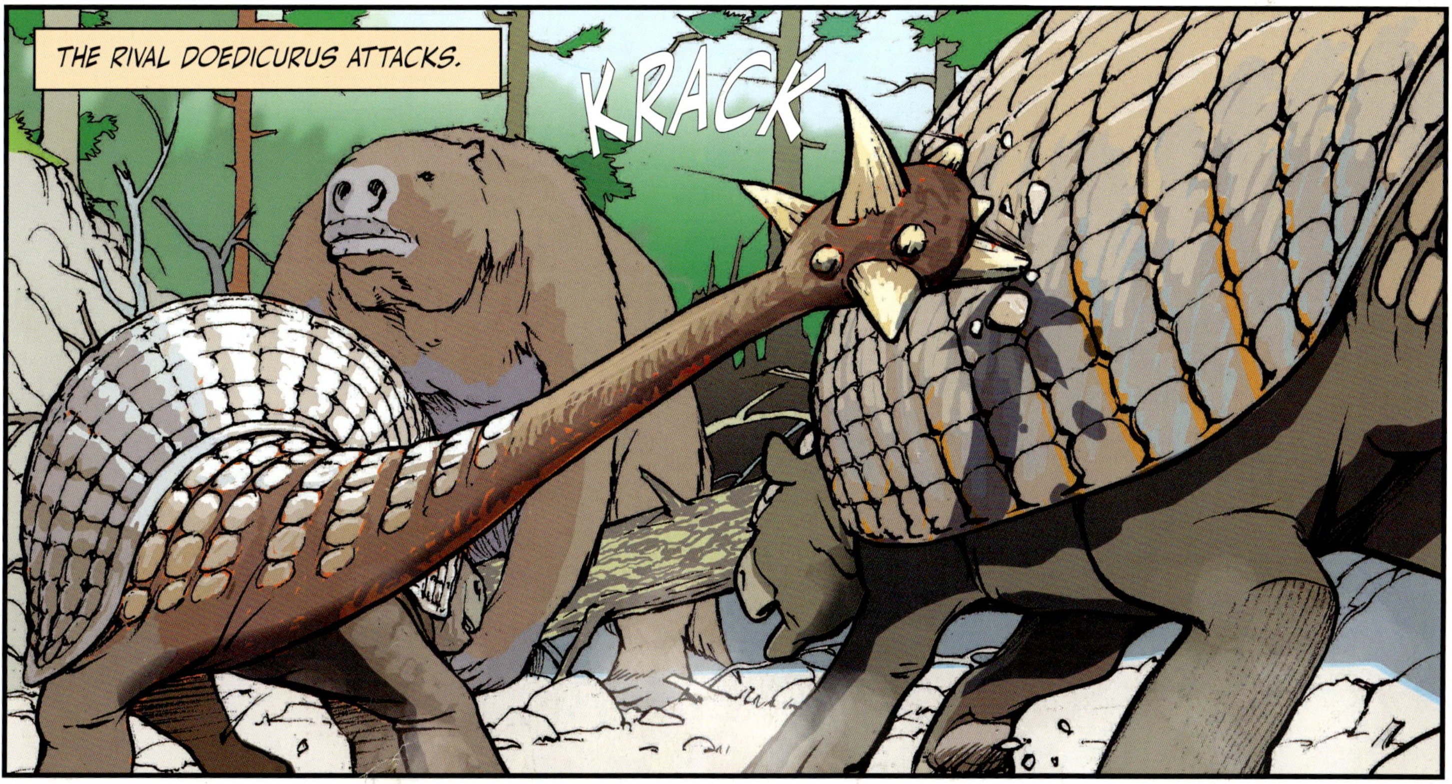
THE RIVAL DOEDICURUS ATTACKS.
KRACK

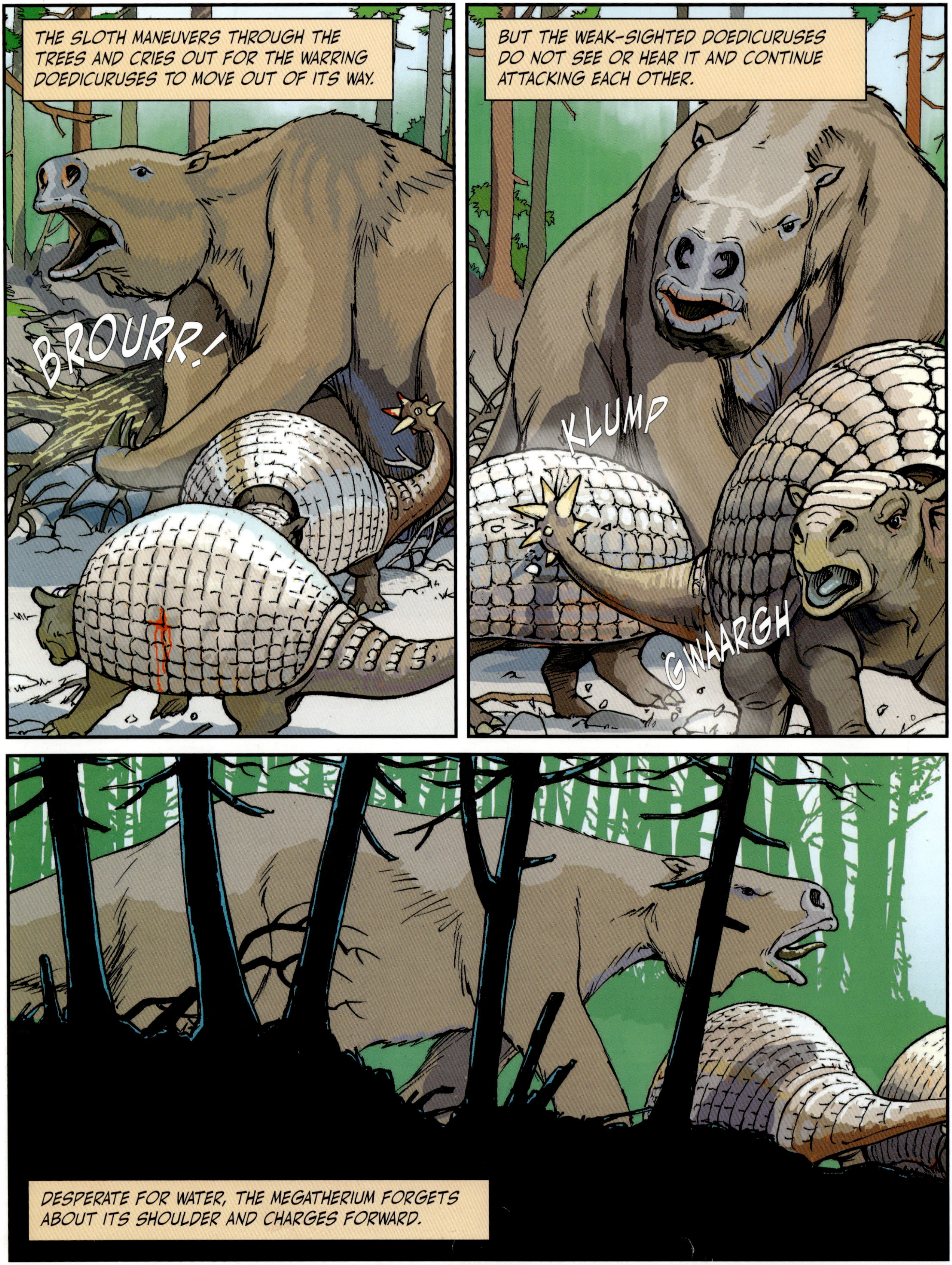
THE SLOTH MANEUVERS THROUGH THE TREES AND CRIES OUT FOR THE WARRING DOEDICURUSES TO MOVE OUT OF ITS WAY.
BROURR!
BUT THE WEAK-SIGHTED DOEDICURUSES DO NOT SEE OR HEAR IT AND CONTINUE ATTACKING EACH OTHER.
KLUMP
GWAARGH
DESPERATE FOR WATER, THE MEGATHERIUM FORGETS ABOUT ITS SHOULDER AND CHARGES FORWARD.

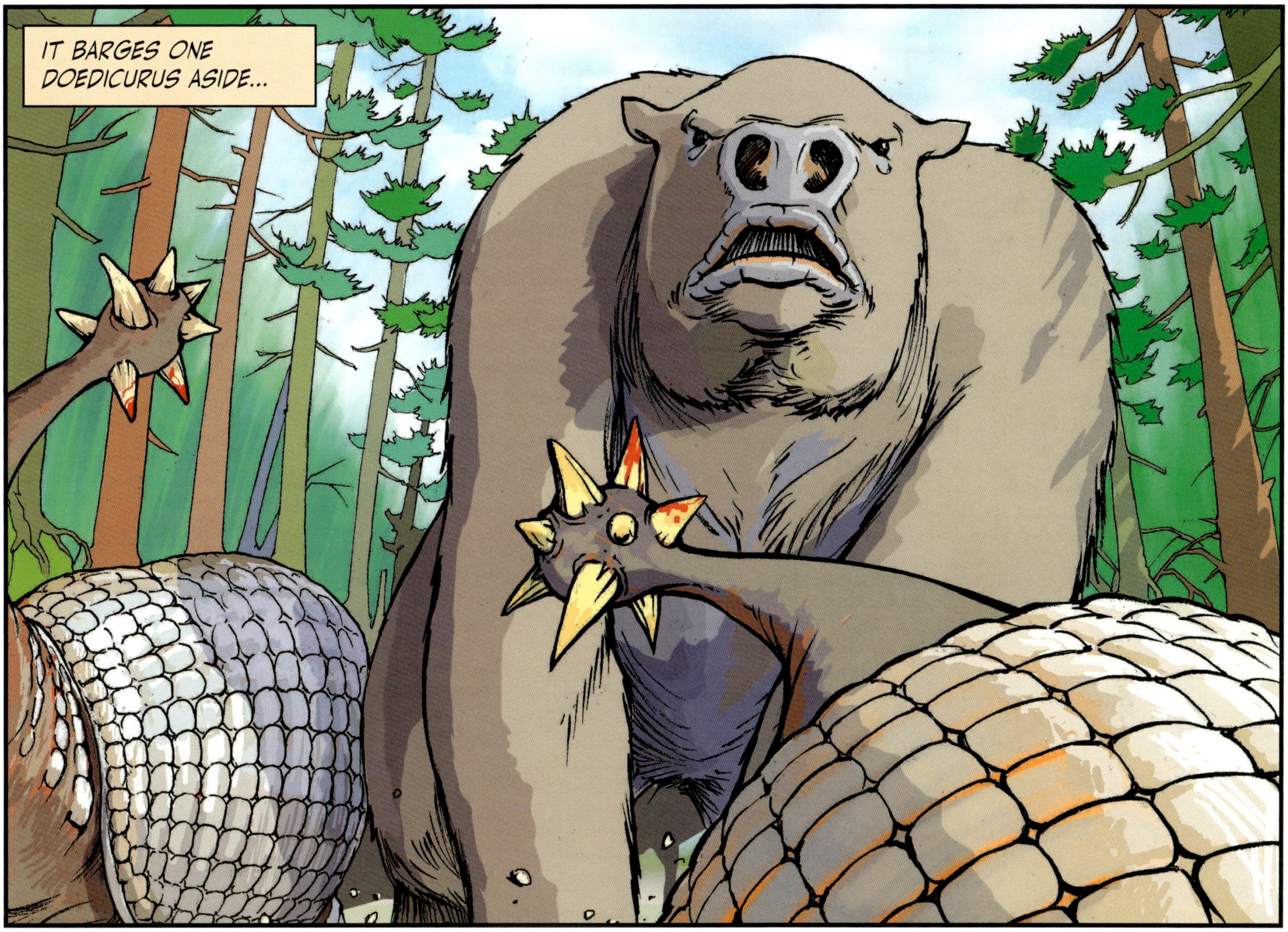
IT BARGES ONE DOEDICURUS ASIDE...

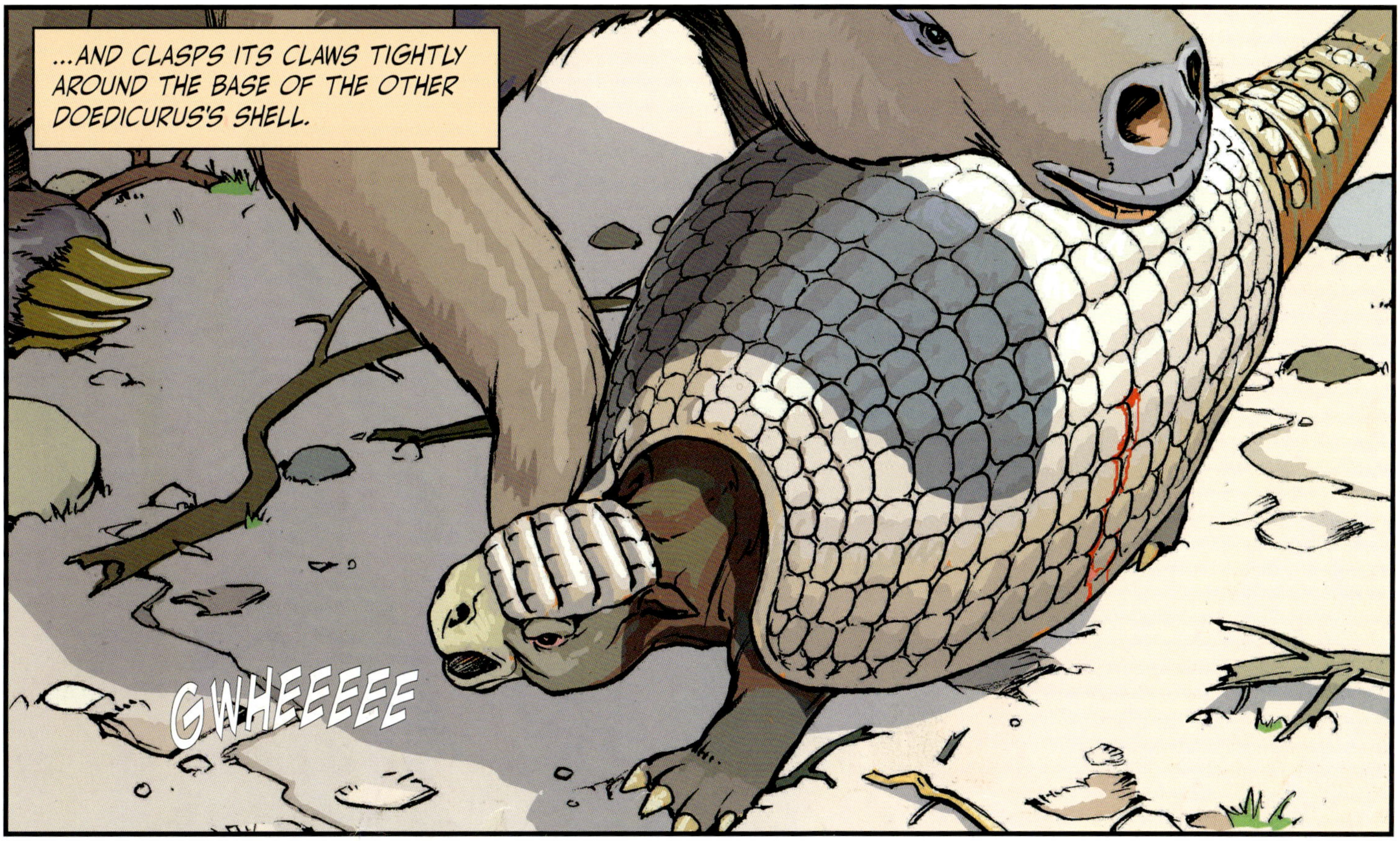
...AND CLASPS ITS CLAWS TIGHTLY AROUND THE BASE OF THE OTHER DOEDICURUS'S SHELL.
GWHEEEEEE

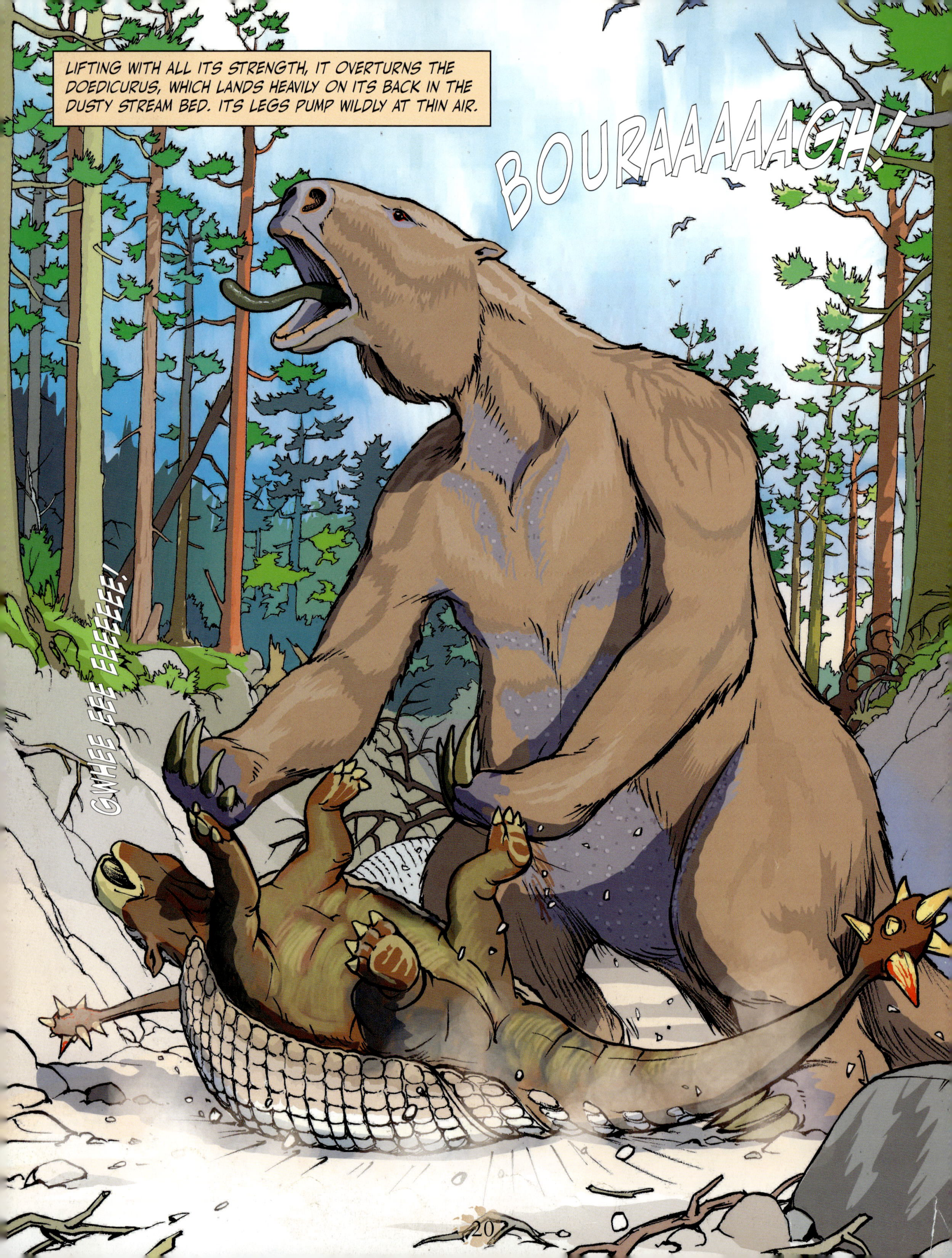

LIFTING WITH ALL ITS STRENGTH, IT OVERTURNS THE DOEDICURUS, WHICH LANDS HEAVILY ON ITS BACK IN THE DUSTY STREAM BED. ITS LEGS PUMP WILDLY AT THIN AIR.
BOURAAAAAAGH!
GWHEE EEE EEEEEEE!

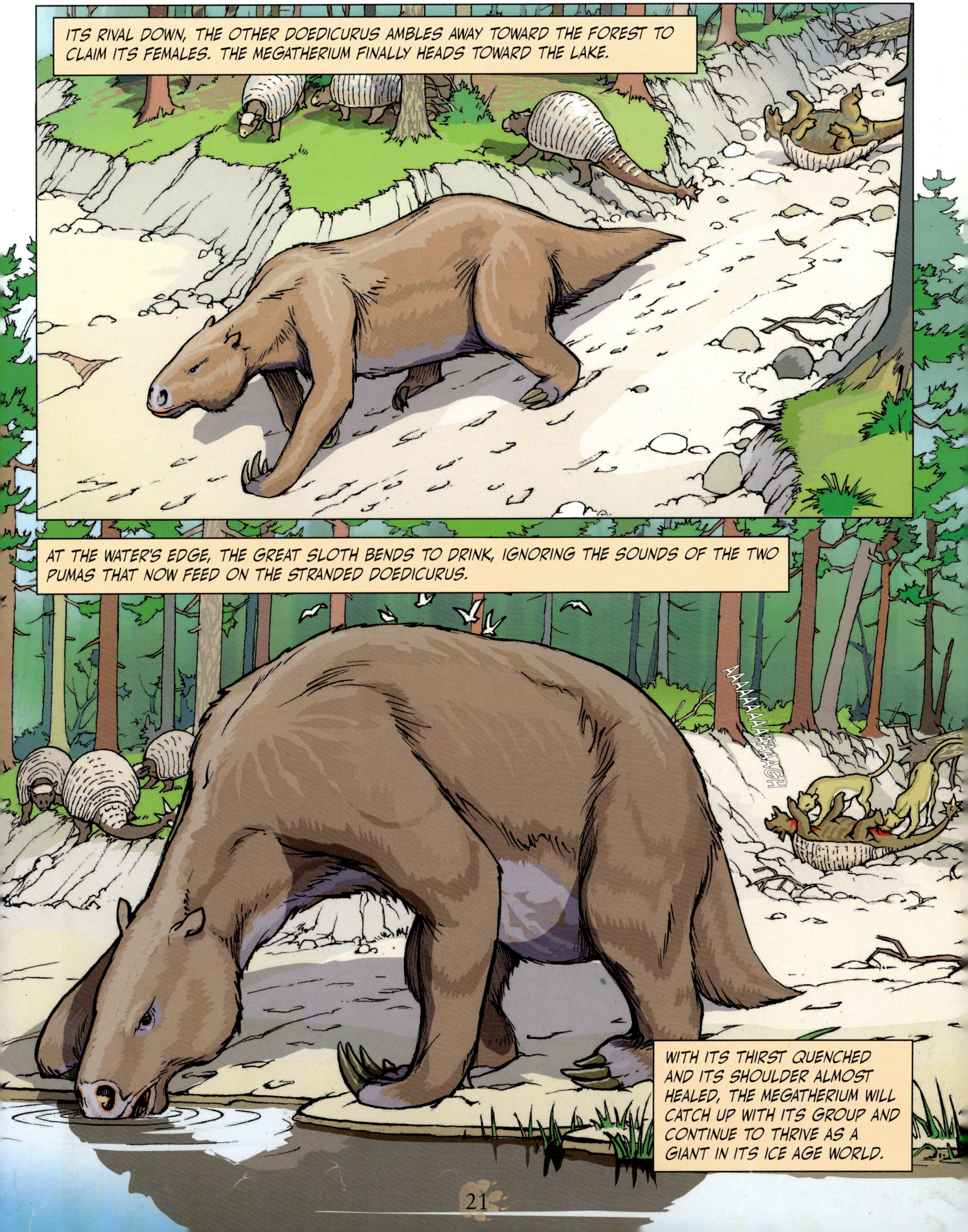
ITS RIVAL DOWN, THE OTHER DOEDICURUS AMBLES AWAY TOWARD THE FOREST TO CLAIM ITS FEMALES. THE MEGATHERIUM FINALLY HEADS TOWARD THE LAKE.
AT THE WATER'S EDGE, THE GREAT SLOTH BENDS TO DRINK, IGNORING THE SOUNDS OF THE TWO PUMAS THAT NOW FEED ON THE STRANDED DOEDICURUS.
AAAAAAAAAAAAAGH
WITH ITS THIRST QUENCHED AND ITS SHOULDER ALMOST HEALED, THE MEGATHERIUM WILL CATCH UP WITH ITS GROUP AND CONTINUE TO THRIVE AS A GIANT IN ITS ICE AGE WORLD.

FOSSIL FINDS

We can get a good idea of what **ANCIENT ANIMALS** may have looked like from their fossils. Fossils are formed when the hard parts of an animal or plant become buried and then turn to rock over millions of years.

Two and a half million years ago, giant sloths moved into North America during the great animal exchange when North and South America joined. The sloths continued to thrive. The largest-ever giant sloth fossil—*Eremotherium* (solitary beast)—was found in the United States, where it would have lived in tropical forest.

Preserved dung and skin from long-dead cave sloths give clues about Megatherium.

The giant sloths became extinct, along with other animals such as sabertooth cats and elephants, when humans arrived in the Americas across a **land bridge** from Europe. Sloths might have been hunted by humans who learned to use spears thrown over long distances.

Megatherium *was the first prehistoric creature to excite real public interest before dinosaurs were discovered.*

ANIMAL GALLERY

All of these **animals** appear in the story.

Palaeolama
height: 4 ft (1.2 m)
a short-haired, camellike browser that had shorter legs than a modern-day llama

Amerhippus
"American horse"
length: 7.2 ft (2.2 m)
a zebralike early true horse that roamed in herds wherever there were grassy plains

Doedicurus
"pestle tail"
length: 4 ft (1.5 m)
largest and best armored of the Glyptodonts (carved tooths), armadillo-like mammals with a long tail

Toxodon
"arched tooth"
length: 8.9 ft (2.7 m)
a common plant eater with the build of a small rhinoceros and a head like a hippopotamus

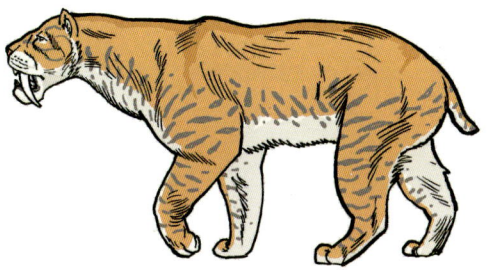

Smilodon Populator
"devasting blade tooth"
length: 8.5 ft (2.6 m)
evolved from the North American sabertooth, this largest and heaviest sabertooth cat had two 12–inch (30–cm) fangs

Stegomastodon platensis
"roof breast tooth wet meadow"
length: 9 ft (2.7 m)
a heavy-set version of a modern-day elephant that browsed shrubs and trees

giant short-faced bear
Arctodus simus
standing height: 8-10 ft (2.4-3 m)
a large, short-backed bear that ate berries, nuts, plants, and scavenged dead animal remains

GLOSSARY

browser a plant eater that feeds on leaves, twigs, and shoots
chainmail armor made of small rings that can stop a sword cutting through it
crown the top part of a tree where the branches grow outward from the trunk
ferment to break down under the action of bacteria
fibrous plant matter made of tough fibers
fossil remains of a living thing that has turned to rock
fractured cracked or broken
land bridge a natural pathway over the sea between two landmasses
low an animal sound made by modern-day cows
lush green, fresh, and moist
osteoderm a hard bony growth in an animal's skin
Pleistocene period time between 1,640,000 to 10,000 years ago marked by a series of great ice ages
predator an animal that naturally preys on others

INDEX

Amerihippuses, 14, 23

browsers, 5

chainmail, 5

Doedicuruses, 17, 19–21, 23

ferment, 4
fractures, 8

giant short-faced bears, 8–9, 23

land bridges, 22
lows, 11

osteoderms, 5

Palaeolamas, 14
Pleistocene period, 4
predators, 5

Smilodon populators, 5, 10, 12, 22–23
Stegomastodon platensises, 4, 23

Toxodons, 10, 13, 23

Lon April 2017 BW May/18

MAR 04 2025 mB